MY CHRISTMAS CRAFT BOOK

MY CHRISTMAS CRAFT BOOK

Anna Murray
Lynda Watts

a Salamander book

Published by Salamander Books Limited
LONDON • NEW YORK

A SALAMANDER BOOK

Published by Salamander Books Ltd.,
129-137 York Way,
London N7 9LG,
England.

ISBN 1 85600 015 X

Distributed by Hodder and Stoughton Services,
PO Box 6, Mill Road, Dunton Green,
Sevenoaks, Kent TN13 2XX.

CREDITS

Managing editor: Veronica Ross
Art director: Rachael Stone
Photographer: Jonathan Pollock
Assistant photographer: Peter Cassidy
Additional designs by: Cheryl Owen
Editor: Coral Walker
Designer: Cherry Randell
Illustrator: John Hutchinson
Character illustrator: Jo Gapper
Diagram artist: Malcolm Porter
Typeset by: Ian Palmer
Colour separation by: Regent Publishing Services Ltd., Hong Kong
Printed in Italy

CONTENTS

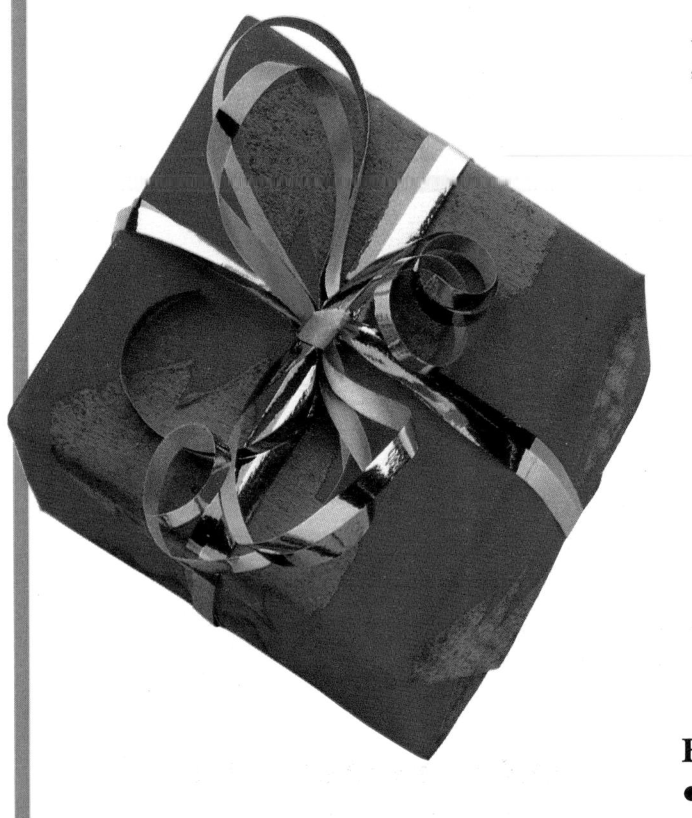

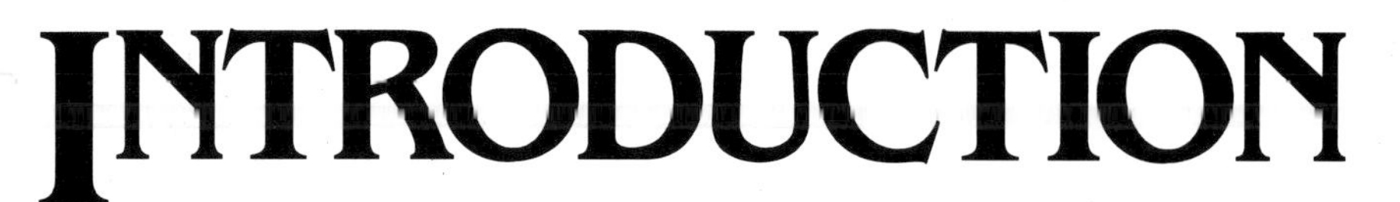

INTRODUCTION

The weeks leading up to Christmas are some of the most exciting of the year, with so much to plan and prepare. In *My Christmas Craft Book* we show you how to make almost everything you will need to make your Christmas really special. There are lots of decorations to make plus party hats, crackers, mobiles and candle holders. We also show you how to make tempting goodies to eat and a range of fun ideas to give as presents.

BEFORE YOU BEGIN

- Do check with an adult before you begin any project.
- Read the instructions first.
- Gather together all the items you need before you begin.
- When using glue or paints, cover your work surface with newspaper or an old cloth.
- Protect your clothes with an apron or wear very old clothes.

WHEN YOU HAVE FINISHED

- Tidy everything away. Store special pens, paints, glue etc in old ice-cream containers or biscuit tins.
- Wash paintbrushes and remember to put the tops back on pens, paints and glue containers.
- If you are baking, put away all the ingredients, wash any dishes and leave the kitchen tidy.

SAFETY FIRST!

You will be able to make most of the projects yourself, but sometimes you will need help. Look out for the SAFETY TIP. It appears on those projects where you will need to ask an adult for help. Remember to use your common sense when using anything hot or sharp, and if in any doubt, ask an adult for advice.

Please remember the basic rules of safety:

- Never leave scissors open or lying around where smaller children can reach them.
- Always stick needles and pins into a pin cushion or a scrap of cloth when you are not using them.
- Never use an oven or a sharp knife without the help or supervision of an adult.

EQUIPMENT & INGREDIENTS

Every project will list all the things you need. Many designs use glitter, shiny paper or tinsel; look among last year's Christmas decorations before buying new materials. Sweets and biscuits will require baking ingredients. You will probably find most of the ingredients you need in the kitchen cupboard, but do check with an adult before taking anything. Some items, such as jewellery fittings or special baking moulds, will need to be bought at large stores or specialist shops.

USING PATTERNS

At the back of the book you will find the patterns you will need to make some of the projects in the book. Using a pencil, trace the pattern you need on to tracing paper. If you are making a project with fabric, cut the pattern out and pin it on to the fabric. Cut out the shape. If you want to cut the pattern out of card, turn your tracing over and rub firmly over the pattern outline with a pencil. The pattern will transfer on to the card. Cut out this shape.

Once you have gained confidence making some of the projects in this book, go on to adapt the ideas to create some of your own designs.

GROWN-UPS TAKE NOTE

Every project in *My Christmas Craft Book* has been designed with simplicity, yet effectiveness, in mind. However, some potentially dangerous items such as an oven or a sharp knife are used for some projects. Your involvement will depend on the ability of the child, but we do recommend that you read through any project before it is undertaken.

FELT TREE ORNAMENTS

Left over braids and scraps of felt can be used to make these cheerful ornaments. Use the shapes shown here or invent your own to suit the materials you have to hand. Snowmen, bells, small Christmas trees or Santa hats are just some other ideas for you to try.

YOU WILL NEED
Card
Fabric glue
Felt in different colours
Glitter
Assortment of braids, ribbons, cord, sequins and lace
Tracing paper and pencil

1 Using a pencil, trace either the boot or the candle pattern on page 84. Turn the tracing over and lay it on to the card. Rub firmly over the outline with a pencil. The pattern will appear on the card. Cut out the shape.

2 To make the boot, coat a large piece of card with glue and stick some felt on to it. Position the boot pattern on the felt and draw around it. Cut out one boot then flip the pattern over to cut out a second boot. Glue trims and sequins in a pattern on to the felt side of one boot.

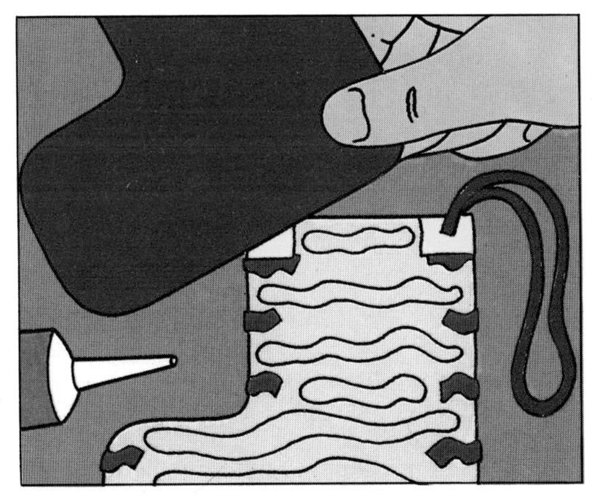

3 Turn the boot over and glue a loop of ribbon or cord to the top. Coat the card with glue and stick the plain felt boot to the decorated one.

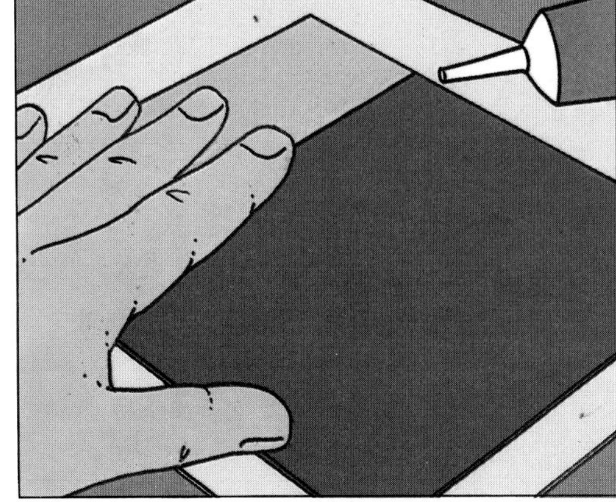

4 To make the candle, glue a strip of felt at least 12cm (4¾in) wide on to card. For the flame, cut a strip of yellow felt at least 4cm (1½in) wide and glue to the card so that it touches the edge of the candle felt.

5 Cut out the candle pattern following the instructions in step 1. Position the pattern on the felt, as shown, so that the flame is on the yellow felt. Draw around the pattern and cut out. Flip the pattern over to cut out a second candle. Decorate and finish off following the instructions in step 3. Sprinkle the flame with glitter to finish.

POP-UP SANTA

Cards that have a pop-up section are expensive to buy, but not that hard to make. Try making several cards so that you can give one to each friend. Make sure you use card and paper that is firm, and not floppy.

1 On the blue card, draw a rectangle 28cm x 18cm (11in x 7in). Draw a line down the centre to divide it into two. Cut out the card and fold it in half.

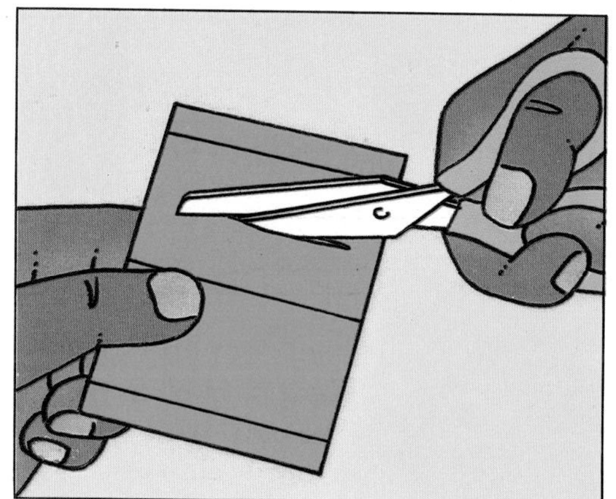

2 Trace the patterns on page 85. Turn the tracings over and lay the body pattern on to red paper, the beard on to white paper, the sack on to brown paper and the chimney on to green. Rub over the outlines with a pencil. The images will appear on the coloured paper. Cut out the patterns and the slot in the chimney.

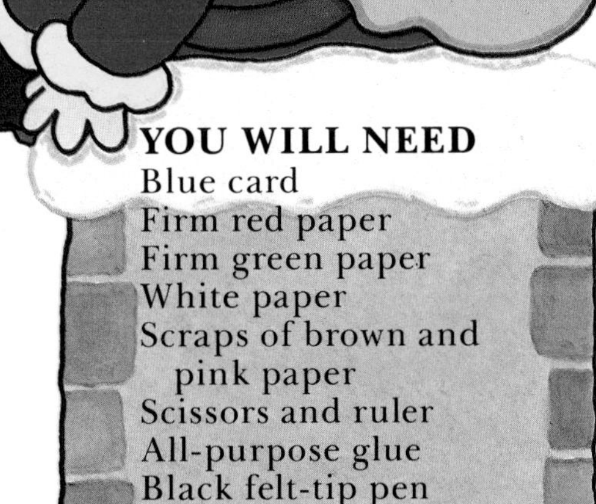

YOU WILL NEED
Blue card
Firm red paper
Firm green paper
White paper
Scraps of brown and pink paper
Scissors and ruler
All-purpose glue
Black felt-tip pen
Tracing paper and pencil

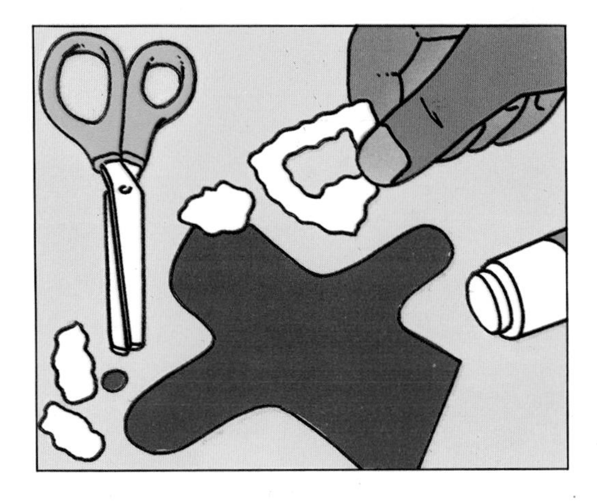

3 Using the body pattern as a guide, cut two cuffs and a pompon from white paper and a face from pink paper. Glue all the shapes on to the body shape. Draw on the eyes and add a red nose.

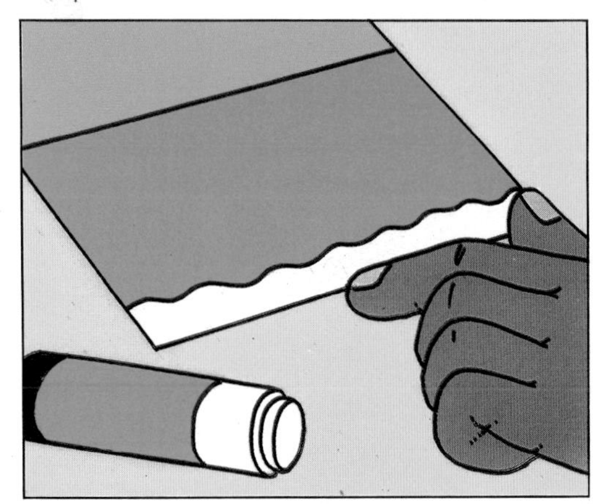

4 To make the roof, draw a rectangle 14cm x 18cm (5½in x 7in) on to green paper and cut it out. Stick it to one half of the inside of the card. Cut some extra white paper to look like snow, and glue one piece to the front of the chimney and one to the edge of the green roof.

5 Fold the chimney into shape as shown, and slip the Santa into the slot. Fold a little of Santa's body down and stick it to the inside of the chimney.

6 Position the chimney and Santa inside the card, as shown. This is how it will look when the card is open. Dab glue on the chimney tabs, then stick it in place.

SALT-DOUGH CANDLE HOLDERS

These sparkling star candle holders are made from salt dough – just flour, salt and water – painted and covered in glitter. Despite the fact they sound edible, they are not!

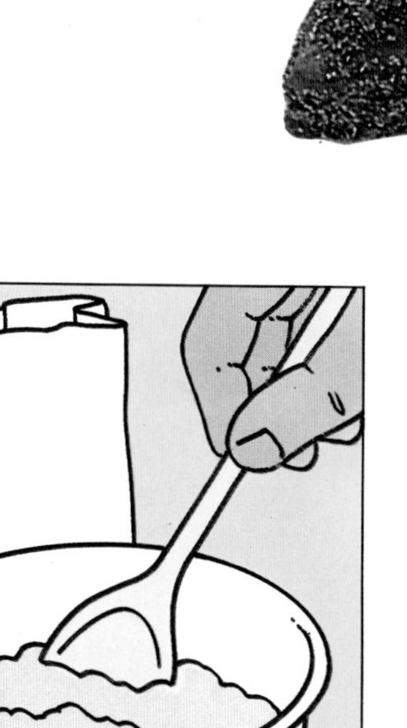

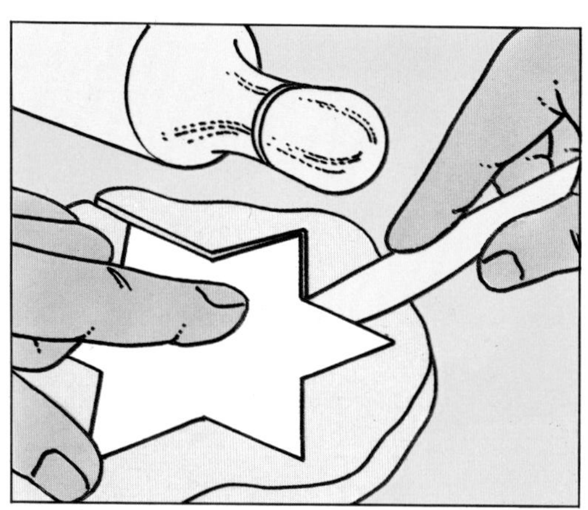

1 Put the flour and salt in the bowl and mix in the water a little at a time until the mixture forms a ball of dough. Sprinkle some extra flour on to your work surface and put the dough in the centre. Roll out the dough until it is about 1.5cm (½in) thick.

2 Turn on the oven to 160°C/ 325°F/Gas mark 3. Using a pencil, trace one of the large star patterns on page 86. Turn the tracing over and lay it on to a piece of card. Rub firmly over the outline with a pencil. The pattern will appear on the card. Cut out the shape. Lay the pattern on the dough and cut around it. Cut out three stars of the same size for each candle holder.

3 Press the base of your candle into two of the stars, then cut this circle away. Carefully place the two stars with the holes in them on to the uncut star, lining up the points. Lift the star on to the baking sheet. Check that the candle still fits. If you prefer, make a round candle holder and decorate it with small star shapes. Trace the small star from the pattern on page 86.

YOU WILL NEED
2 cups plain flour
1 cup salt
1 cup water
Mixing bowl and wooden spoon
Blunt knife and baking tray
Rolling pin and oven gloves
Poster paints and paintbrush
Glitter
All-purpose glue
Tracing paper and pencil
Scrap card
Candles

SAFETY TIP: *Make sure an adult helps you when using the oven.*

4 Bake the candle holders for about 30 minutes. Wearing oven gloves, remove them from the oven. Once cooled, put the holders on to paper and paint them with poster paints.

5 When the paint has dried, apply glue all over the holder, and sprinkle with glitter. Do not move the holder until the glue has dried.

CHRISTMAS STOCKING

This Christmas, make a special stocking to put beside the fire, or use it as a novelty bag for small presents. Use a glue stick for this project, as any of the wetter glues may make the colour run in the crêpe paper.

YOU WILL NEED

Double-sided crêpe paper
Thick sewing thread and needle
Tracing paper and pencil
Scraps of white, black and coloured card
Scissors
Pins
Glue stick and pen

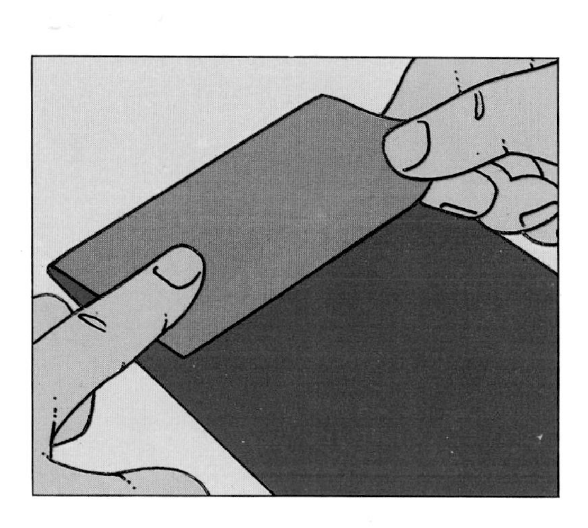

1 Using a pencil, trace the stocking pattern on page 87. Cut out the pattern and pin to a piece of crêpe paper which has been folded in half. Carefully cut round the pattern to give two stocking shapes. Fold down the top of the stockings to show the second colour of crêpe paper.

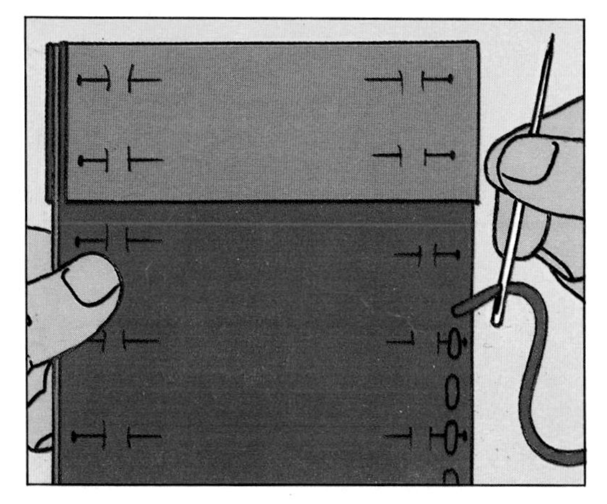

2 Pin the stockings together and, using the needle and thread, sew around the outer edge, as shown above.

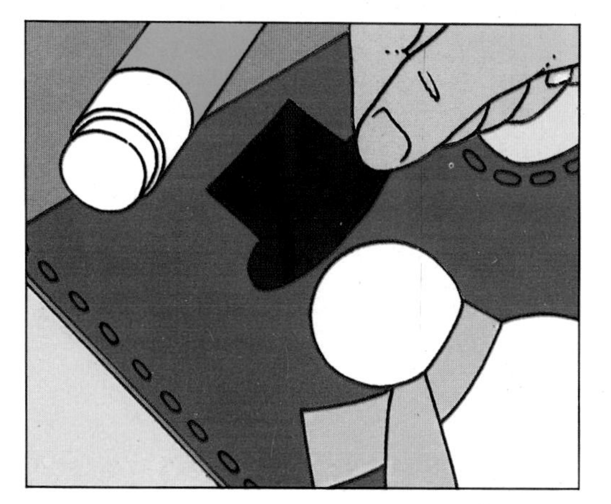

3 Cut a snowman shape from white paper and stick it in place on the stocking. Cut a hat from black paper and a scarf from a different colour. Glue them on to the snowman.

4 Cut a small carrot shape for the nose and circles for buttons and glue them on. Trim the hat with some holly leaves cut from green paper and berries from red. Draw dots for the eyes with the pen.

POT-POURRI SACHETS

These little sachets, filled with perfumed pot-pourri, make wonderful gifts. You can also hang them from the Christmas tree to give the room a beautiful smell. Look out for special Christmas pot-pourri which smells of oranges, pine and cinnamon.

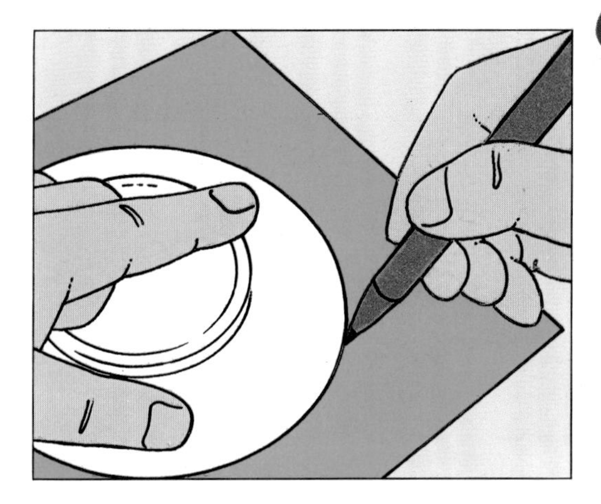

1 Lay out the fabric, wrong side facing you. Place the plate on the fabric and draw around it with the pen. Using the pinking shears, cut out the circle, just inside the pen line.

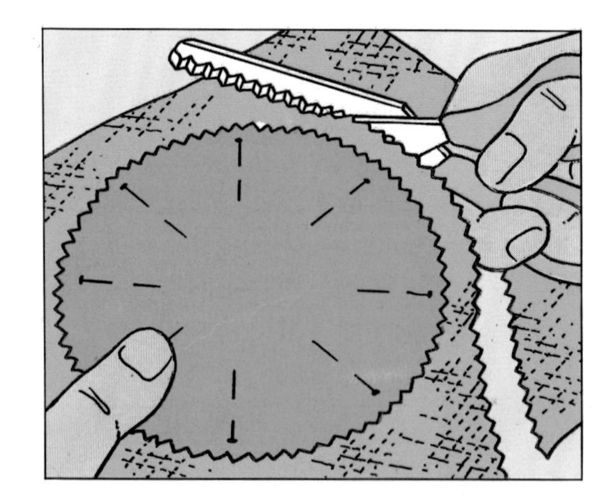

2 Pin the fabric circle to two pieces of net. Using pinking shears, cut out two slightly larger net circles. Lay the fabric circle down, wrong side facing you. Place the two net circles on top.

3 Pour a small mound of pot-pourri into the centre of the circles. Gather the circles up around the pot-pourri and tightly wrap an elastic band around the fabric. Frill the fabric out at the top.

4 Decorate the sachets with a ribbon bow. Add other trims, like wired beads, poking the ends of the wire around behind the ribbon. You could stitch or glue a few sequins to the bow as well.

YOU WILL NEED

Printed cotton fabric
Coloured net
Pot-pourri
Scissors, pinking shears and pins
Elastic bands
Ribbons
Wired baubles, berries and sequins
Pen and a small plate

PAPER LANTERNS

Brighten up those dark Christmas evenings with a colourful paper lantern. Put glitzy metallic paper inside to make it look warm and welcoming. You can make one large lantern, or you can string lots of small ones together to make a festive garland.

1 Fold the paper square in half. Then fold back the two edges as shown.

2 Cut equally spaced slits along the paper from the centre fold to the narrow folds at the edge. Cut away one slit from one end. Unfold the paper, leaving the two narrow folds in place. Between each slit, cut a diamond shape into the narrow fold, as shown.

YOU WILL NEED

Brightly coloured paper squares
Glue stick
Thin gold metallic paper
Pencil
Scissors

3 Take the gold paper and cut a piece as wide as the coloured paper square, but slightly shorter. Stick the gold paper to the wrong side of the coloured square along both long edges.

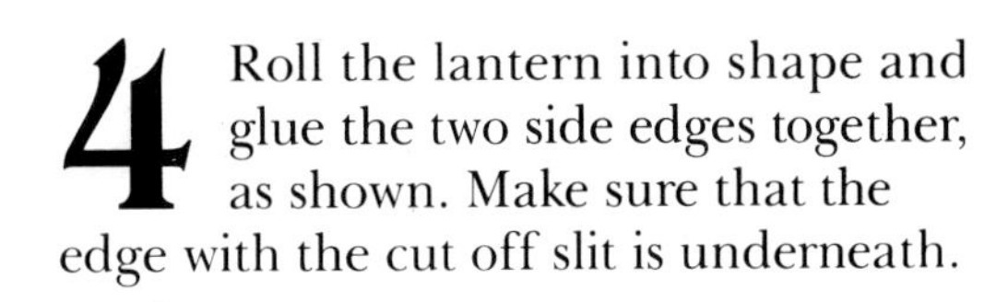

4 Roll the lantern into shape and glue the two side edges together, as shown. Make sure that the edge with the cut off slit is underneath.

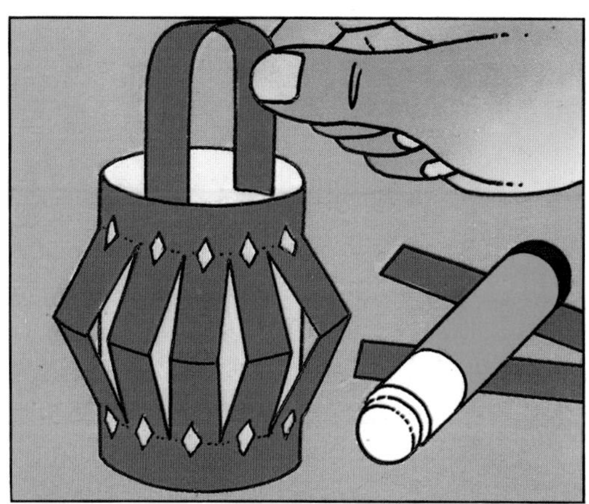

5 Cut two strips of coloured paper to make a handle. Glue them together and to the opposite inside edges of the lantern.

SHINY STARS

These pretty stars are made from coloured beads threaded on to wire. The beads sparkle in the light and make lovely ornaments.

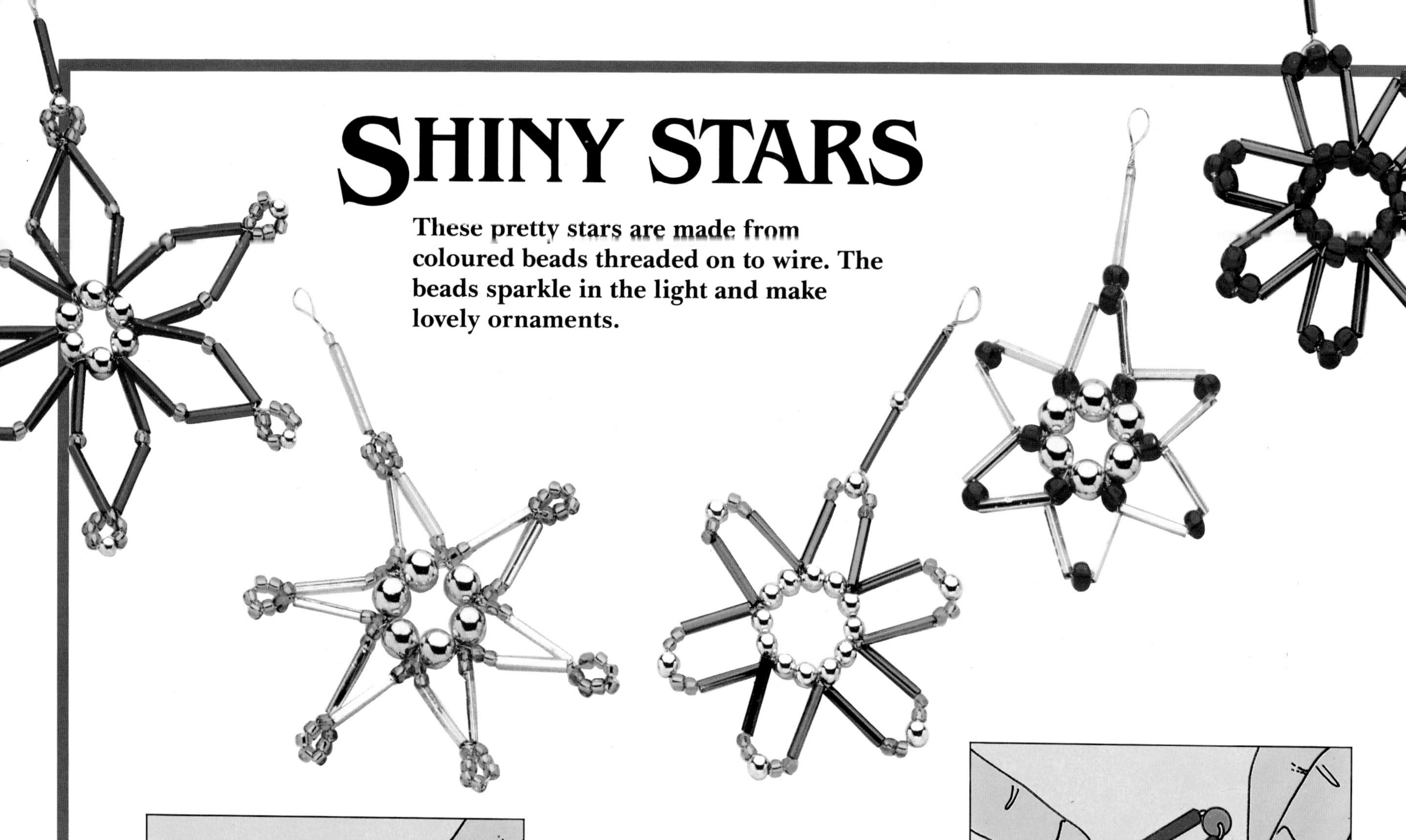

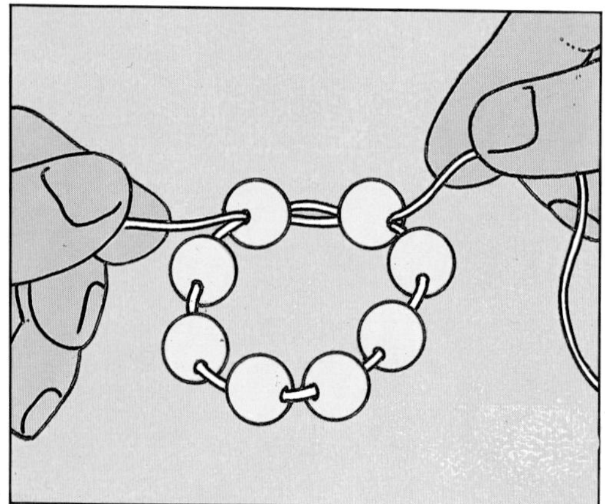

1 Cut a length of wire about 60cm (2ft) long. Thread the larger round beads on to the centre of the wire and push one end of the wire back into the holes of two or three beads. Pull both ends of the wire tight to form a circle of beads.

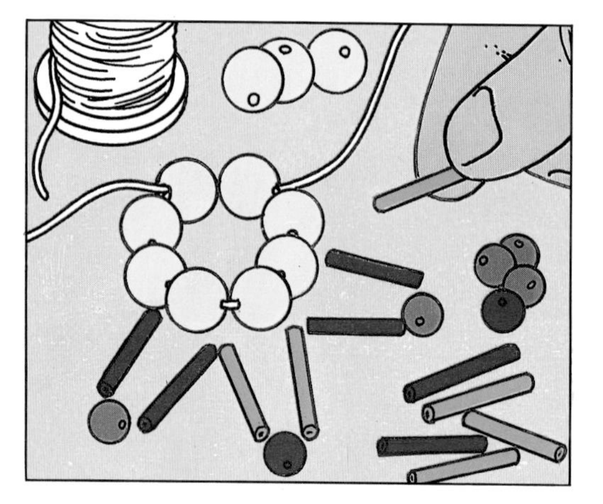

2 Lay the circle down and arrange some of the other beads in 'V' shapes around it – these beads form the arms of the stars. When you are happy with your design, proceed.

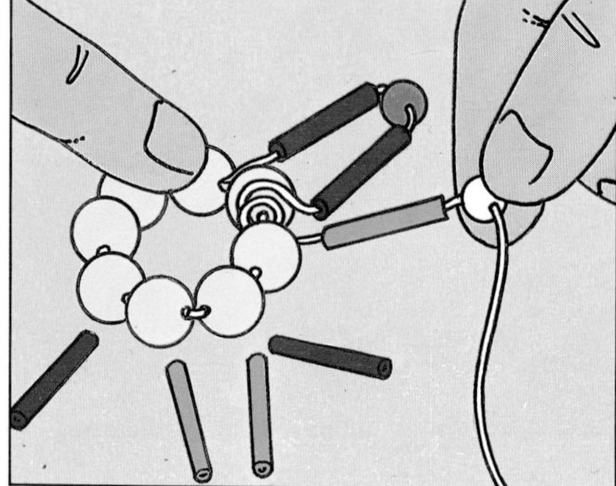

3 Working with one loose end of wire, thread the beads from one 'V' shape, in your chosen order. Bend the 'V' into shape and wrap the loose end of wire in between the next two large beads of the circle to secure it.

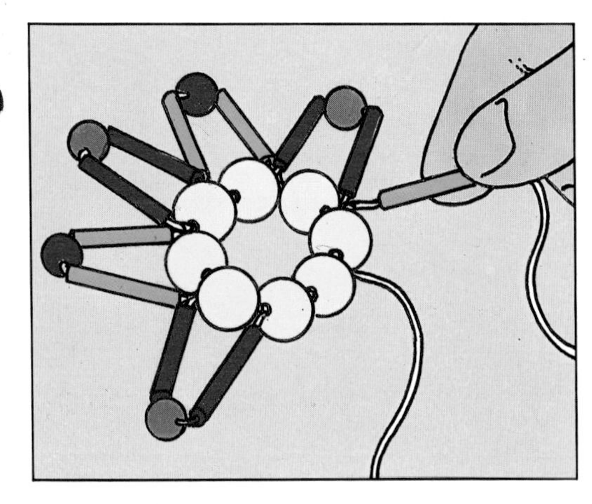

4 Thread the next 'V' shape of beads on to the remaining wire and secure them as before. Continue until all the beads are threaded. You may need to use the other end of the wire, if the first becomes too short. When the star is complete, wrap the ends of the wire between some beads and trim.

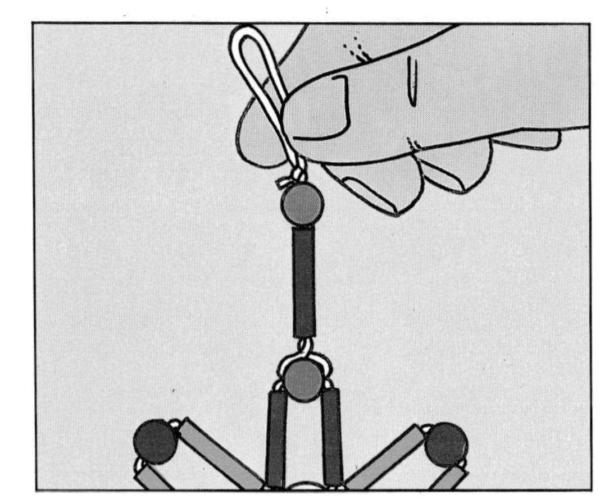

5 Make a hanging loop by threading a short length of wire, through one of the beads at the point of a 'V'. Fold it double, then thread a long bead on to it, and a small round one. Twist the wire into a loop, as shown, and push the ends back down into the beads. To make a selection of star ornaments, copy the designs shown on these pages.

YOU WILL NEED

Round beads about 6mm (¼in) in diameter
Long beads
Other assorted beads
Spool of beading wire
Scissors

RAFFIA WREATH

One of the friendliest Christmas traditions is to hang a festive wreath on the front door. Not only does it cheer up passers-by but it gives a very warm welcome to family and friends.

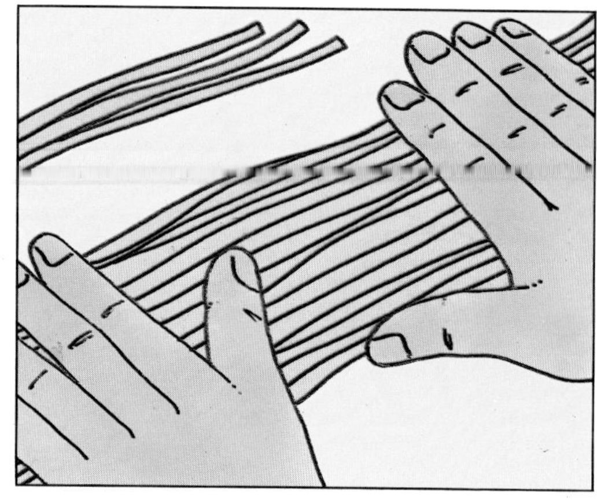

1 Lay the raffia on some paper and smooth it out as shown. Put a few single lengths of raffia to one side to use as ties. Tie the raffia into a bunch at one end.

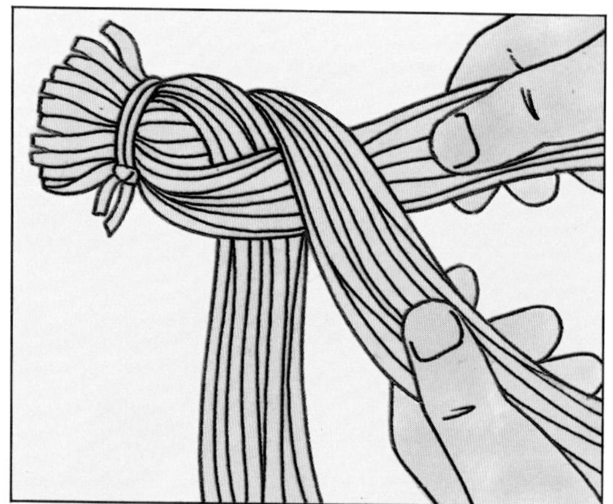

2 Divide the raffia into three bundles and plait it as you would hair, taking the outer bunches over the centre one. When the plait is complete, tie it firmly at one end with one of the extra pieces of raffia. Trim both ends of the plait.

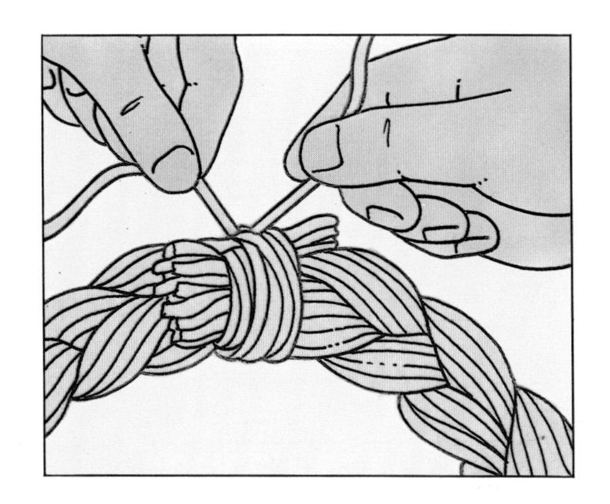

3 Curve the plait into a circle and overlap the ends. Tie them together with raffia, wrapping it round and round the join to completely cover it. Make a firm knot and trim the ends.

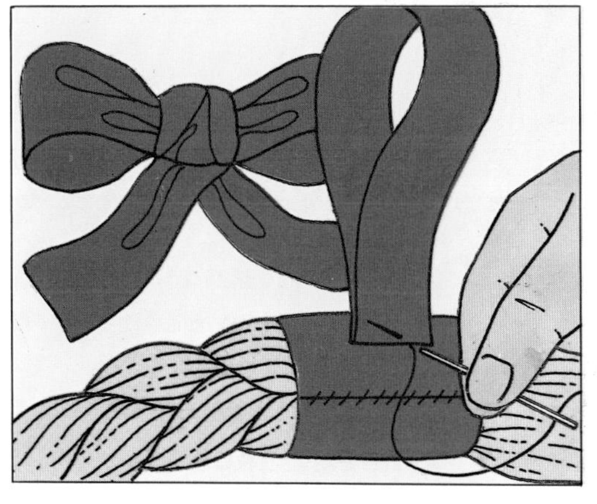

4 Cut a 20cm (8in) length of wide ribbon and wrap it over the join, stitching it at the back. Cut another piece of ribbon about 30cm (12in) long, fold it into a loop and stitch it to the back of the wreath. Tie the remaining ribbon into a bow and stitch it to the front.

YOU WILL NEED

- Raffia
- Florists' or fuse wire
- 1m (1yd) of wide ribbon
- Narrow ribbons
- Gold acrylic paint and paintbrush
- Pine cones
- Cinnamon sticks
- Needle and thread
- Extra trims like wired berries and leaves (sold at Christmas time)

5 Prepare the wired decorations. To wire pine cones, cut a short length of wire and wrap it around the base of the cone, twisting the ends together. Wire cinnamon sticks into small bunches and hide the wire with a ribbon tie. Shop bought trims should have wires already attached.

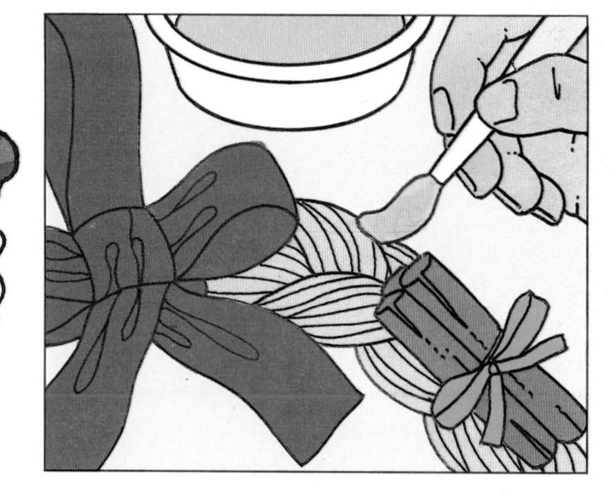

6 Press the ends of the wired decorations through to the back of the wreath and twist them into the plait to secure them. When the decoration is complete, paint the wreath with dabs of gold paint.

SAFETY TIP: *Ask an adult to help you to prepare the wired decorations.*

FESTIVE FRIDGE MAGNETS

These merry Christmas fridge badges will cheer up anyone working hard in the kitchen during the festive season. They are great fun to make using coloured modelling clay that is baked in the oven.

1 Roll out some green and red clay, about 6mm (¼in) thick. Using a blunt knife, cut out some tree shapes from the green clay and cut squares from the red clay.

2 To decorate the tree, roll out yellow clay and cut out a star shape. To make the baubles, roll red pieces of clay between your finger and thumb. Press the decorations on to the tree. For the parcels, roll out some blue clay and cut out strips for the ribbons and bows. Press on to the parcel.

3 Bake the clay shapes in an oven following the instructions on the packet. Wearing oven gloves, remove the shapes from the oven. Leave to cool and harden.

4 Glue a small fridge magnet to the back of each shape. Let the glue dry before using.

YOU WILL NEED
- Modelling clay that will harden in the oven
- Blunt knife
- Rolling pin
- Fridge magnets
- All-purpose glue
- Baking sheet
- Oven gloves

SAFETY TIP: *Make sure an adult helps you when using the oven.*

FABRIC CUT-OUT CARDS

Delight your family and friends by making your own designer Christmas cards. Simply cut 'windows' into coloured card and then use festive fabrics for decoration.

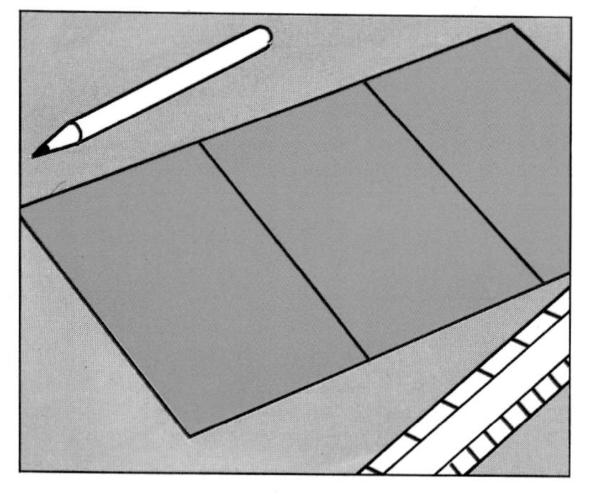

1 With a pencil and ruler draw a rectangle on to a piece of card 12cm x 30cm (4¾in x 12in); cut it out. Divide the card into three equal sections. Mark the sections with a pencil.

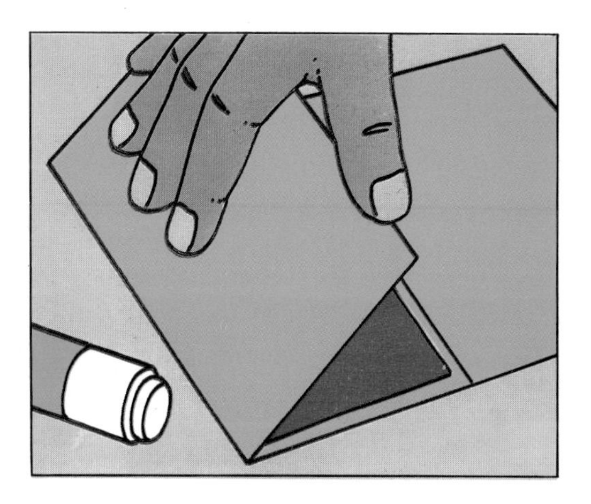

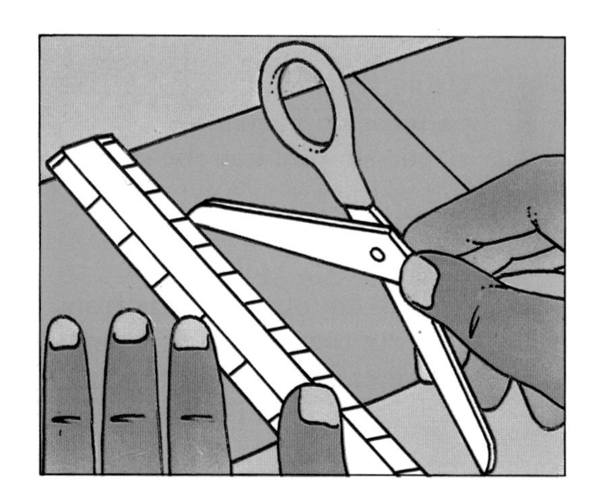

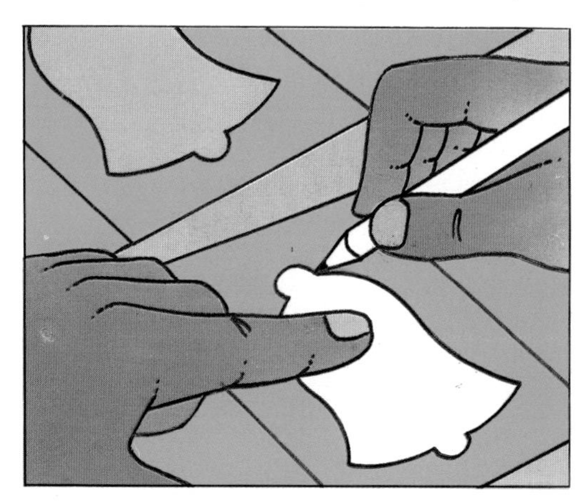

2 Lightly score along the pencil lines using a ruler and scissor points. Ask an adult to help you do this.

3 Using a pencil, trace either the bell or the tree shape on page 88. Turn the tracing over and lay on to a piece of scrap card. Rub firmly over the outline with a pencil. The pattern will appear on the card. Cut out the shapes. Place the pattern on to the centre section of the card. Draw around it and cut out the shape to make a 'window' in the card.

4 With the inside of the card facing you, arrange one piece of fabric or several overlapping pieces behind the cut-out shape. Make sure the fabric is right-side down. Glue the fabric to the card.

5 Cover the inside of the left-hand section of the card with glue. Fold it over, as shown, and stick firmly to the centre section to cover the fabric.

SAFETY TIP: *Make sure an adult helps you when using sharp scissors.*

CRÊPE PAPER TREE

This tree is designed to sit on a table or desk. The leaves are made from frills of crêpe paper, stuck into a cardboard cone. Once you have made it, decorate it like a proper tree, using miniature trims.

1 Using a pencil, trace the patterns on page 89. Cut out all the shapes. Lay the cone pattern on to the green card and hold it in place with masking tape. Cut around the pattern. Follow these instructions to cut out two stars from white card. Pin the frill patterns on to the crêpe paper, and cut out about 30 of each of the three frill shapes.

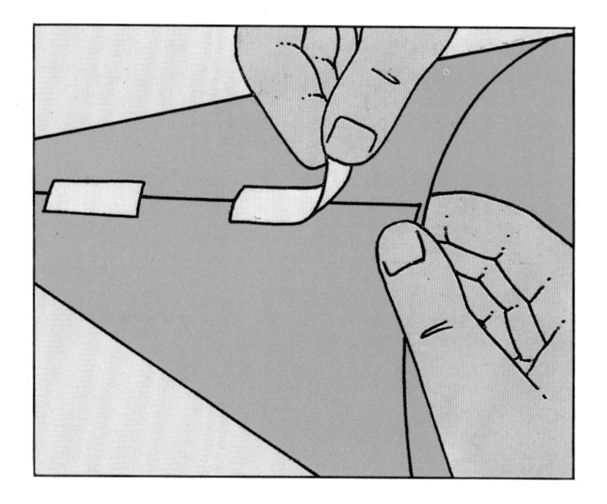

2 Roll up the cone. Overlap the straight edges slightly and stick together with masking tape. Put tape on the inside join too.

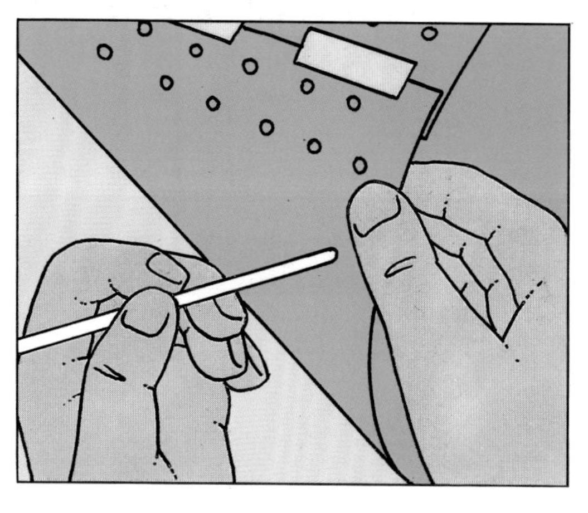

3 Using a skewer, punch rows of holes into the cone. The holes should be about 5cm (2in) apart. Make the holes closer together at the top of the tree, so they are about 12mm (½in) apart.

4 Scrunch up the narrow ends of the frills and wrap a small piece of tape around them. Push these taped ends into the holes, placing the largest frills at the base of the cone, the medium-sized ones in the middle and the smallest ones at the top.

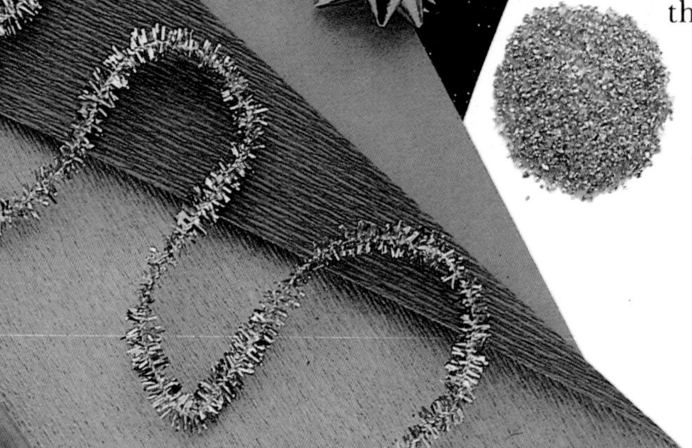

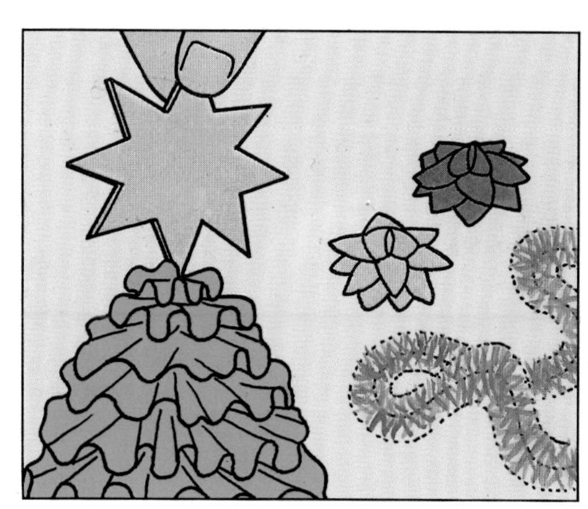

5 Lay the stars on the newspaper and cover one side of each one with glue. Sprinkle gold glitter over the stars. When the glue has dried, glue the two stars together, glitter sides out. Push one point of the star into the hole in the top of the tree. Decorate with tinsel and bows.

FLYING ANGELS

Hang this cute mobile in a doorway, or from the corner of a room. If you don't want to make a complete mobile, the individual angels can be used as Christmas tree ornaments.

1 Using a pencil, trace the dress pattern on page 90. Cut out the pattern and pin to the crêpe paper. Cut out the dress then fold it in half along the foldline and cut away the neck hole. Fold the tabs back and glue them down. Glue the edges of the sleeves together.

2 Thread the needle with gold wool and sew round the neck opening, leaving long ends of thread.

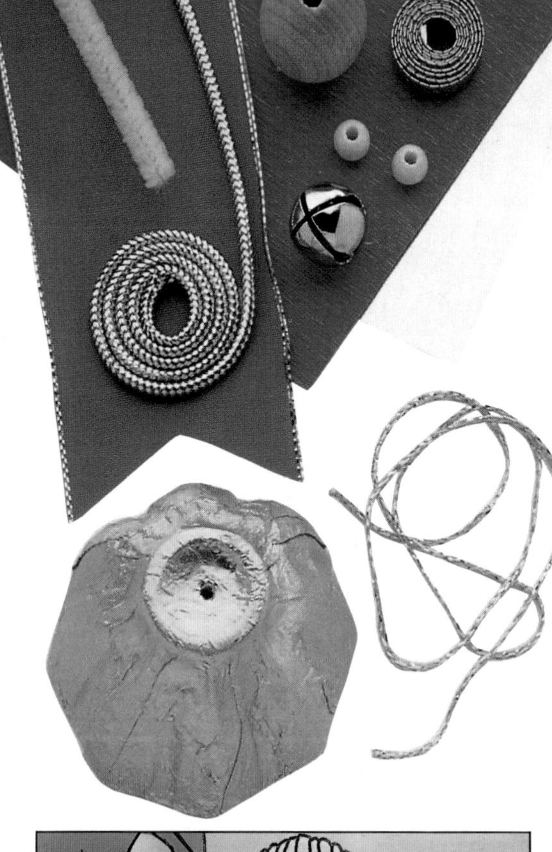

3 Paint a face on a large bead. Cut the gold wool into pieces about 2cm (¾in) long and glue them to the head for hair.

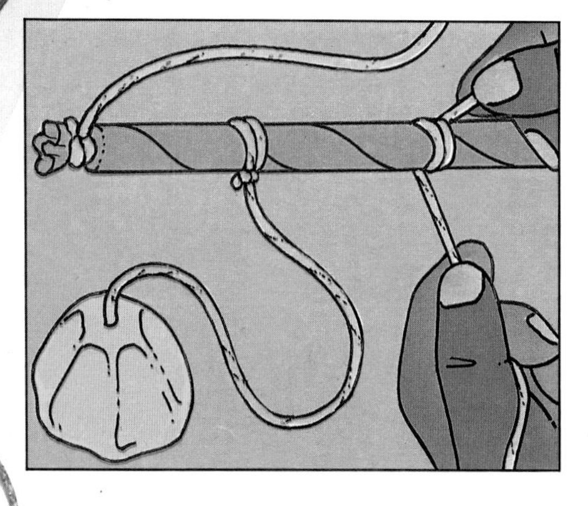

6 Wrap ribbon around the stick and glue the ends in place. Cut the gold cord into four lengths. Tie one piece to the ends of the stick, so that the mobile can hang up. Make three gold bells following the instructions given for Bell Pendant on pages 40 and 41. Tie each bell on to a length of cord, then tie the bells on to the stick. Hang the angels by folding their pipe cleaner hands over the cord.

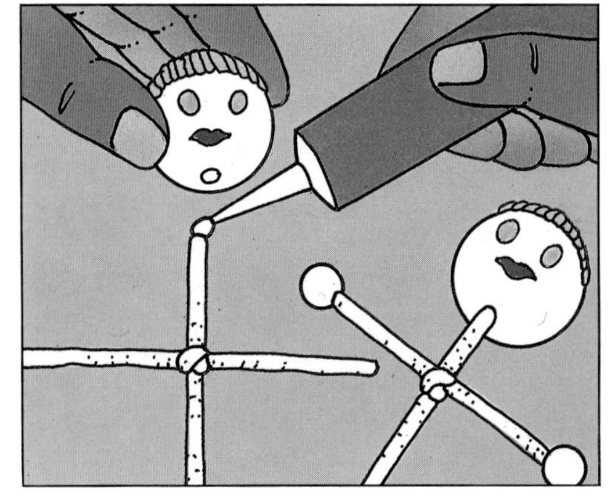

4 For the body, cut a pipe cleaner in half and twist the two pieces together as shown. Dab glue on to the ends of the arms and push on the small beads. Dab glue on to the neck and push on the head. Put the dress on to the body. Pull the thread ends tightly round the neck and tie them into a bow.

5 Using a pencil, trace the wing pattern on page 90. Turn the tracing paper over and lay it on the back of the gold card. Rub firmly over the outline with a pencil. The pattern will appear on the card. Cut out one wing. Now lay the shape back on the gold card. Draw around it and cut out another wing shape. Glue the shapes together and stick them on the back of the angel. Make three angels in this way.

YOU WILL NEED

Crêpe paper
3 large white beads
6 small white beads
3 pipe cleaners
Gold wool and needle
Gold card
Stick 30cm (1ft) long
1m (1yd) of ribbon
1.5m (1½yd) of gold cord
All-purpose glue and scissors
Poster paints and paintbrush

CHRISTMAS MOBILE

Cut Christmas motifs, such as stars, moons and bells, from thick corrugated card. Simply paint the shapes with bright, glittery paint and decorate them with ribbons and sequins to make a delightful Christmas mobile.

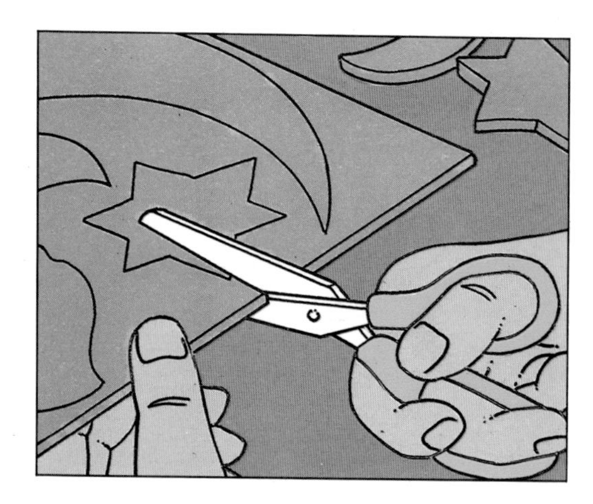

1 Draw various small Christmas shapes on to the corrugated card and one large crescent moon to hang the other shapes from. Cut the shapes out.

YOU WILL NEED

Thick corrugated card
Pen or pencil
Scissors
Gold acrylic paint
Glitter paints
Sequin braid
Patterned ribbon
All-purpose glue
Paint brush
Gold cord

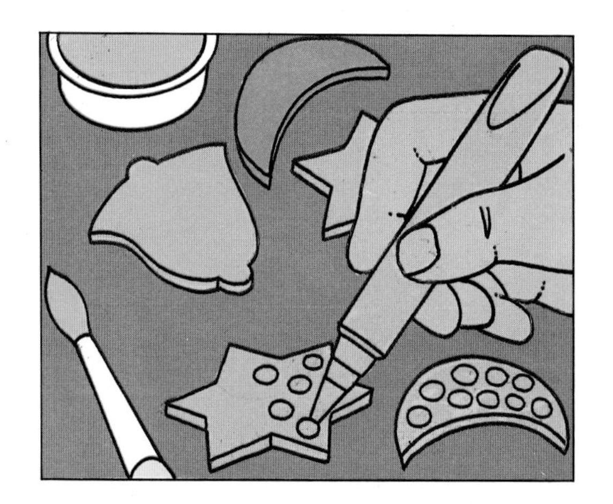

2 Paint all the shapes with gold paint. Leave to dry before adding dabs of glitter paint.

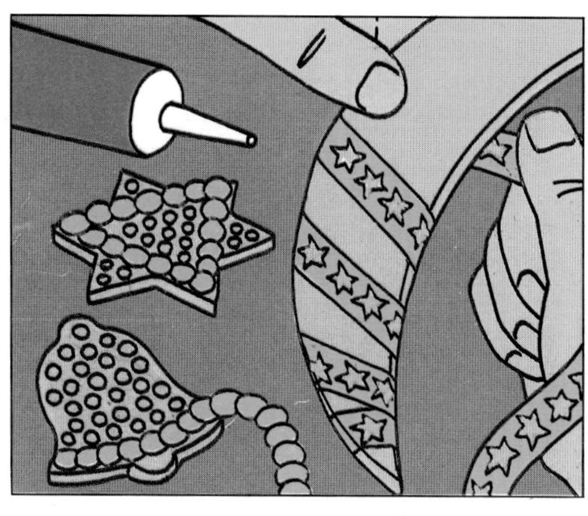

3 Glue the sequin braid on to the smaller painted shapes as shown. Then wrap the ribbon round the large crescent moon, securing the ends in place with glue.

4 Cut one long piece of gold cord to make the hanging loop at the top of the mobile. Cut shorter pieces of cord to go between the smaller shapes. Attach the cord to the shapes by tucking and glueing the ends inside the hollows of the card.

PING PONG BAUBLES

No one would guess these stunning baubles are made from ping pong balls. You can use paint, glitter and a few trimmings to make bright and colourful patterns, and baubles that will make any Christmas tree shine.

1 Use the darning needle to make a hole through the top and bottom of the ping pong ball. Ask an adult to help you do this. Push a wooden skewer through the holes – this will stop the ball from moving while you are decorating it.

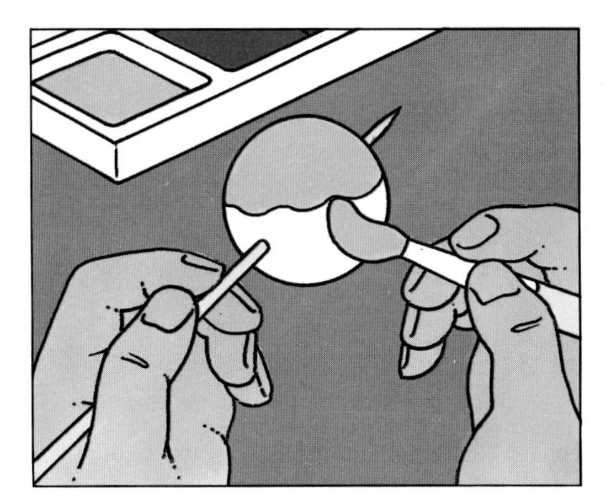

2 Paint the ping pong balls in bright colours. Leave to dry. If the first coat of paint looks a bit patchy, add another coat. Leave the paint to dry completely.

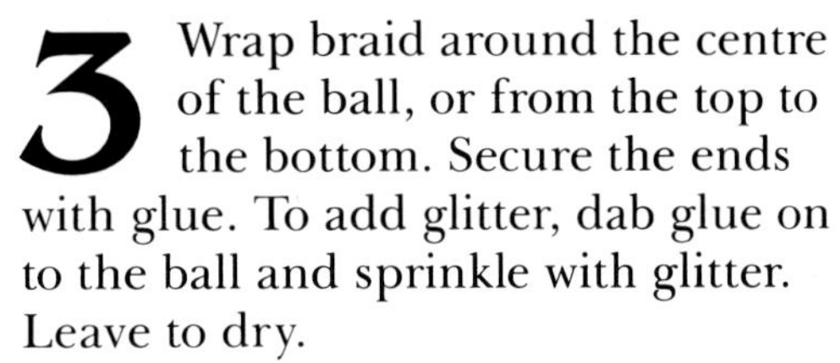

3 Wrap braid around the centre of the ball, or from the top to the bottom. Secure the ends with glue. To add glitter, dab glue on to the ball and sprinkle with glitter. Leave to dry.

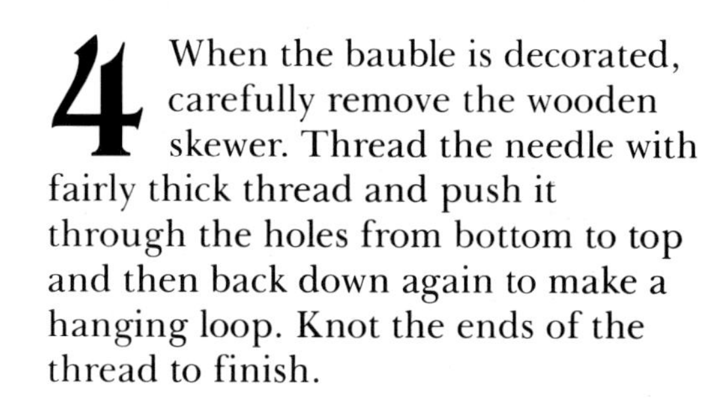

4 When the bauble is decorated, carefully remove the wooden skewer. Thread the needle with fairly thick thread and push it through the holes from bottom to top and then back down again to make a hanging loop. Knot the ends of the thread to finish.

3-D GIFT TAGS

Add a special touch to Christmas parcels by matching the gift tag to the paper. When making 3-D gift tags, it is best to choose wrapping paper with a repeat pattern that has a clear outline to cut around.

1 Roughly cut out four identical motifs from the giftwrap. Glue the motifs to a sheet of paper to make them stiffer.

2 Now, carefully cut around three of the motifs following the outline of the shape. From the fourth motif, cut out separate features, such as Santa's face.

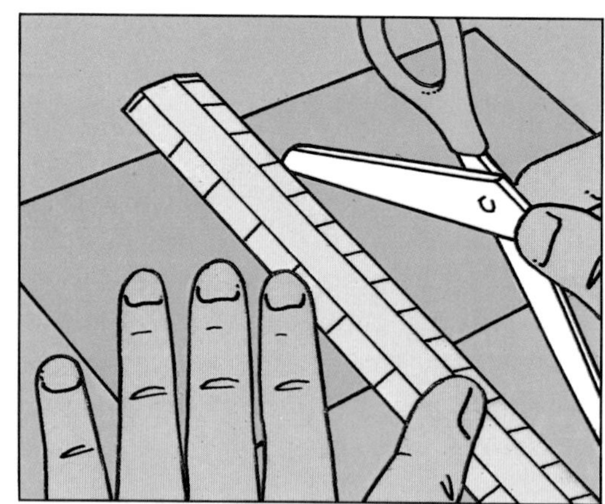

3 Cut a piece of card slightly taller than your chosen motif and at least twice as wide. Score down the centre of the card with a ruler and scissors to make a fold line.

SAFETY TIP: *Make sure an adult helps you when using sharp scissors.*

YOU WILL NEED
Coloured card
Giftwrap with repeat pattern
Scissors
Glue stick
Plain paper
Ruler
Double-sided sticky pads
Hole punch

4 Turn the card over and glue the first motif to the right-hand side. Position sticky pads all over the motif. Put the second motif on top of the first so that it sticks to the pads. Repeat for the third motif.

5 Fix the smaller sections from the fourth motif in the appropriate places using the sticky pads to create a 3-D effect. Fold the card in half and punch a hole in the top left hand corner. Thread with ribbon.

MR FROSTY

Make a jolly Mr Frosty snowman using scraps of felt, for a Christmas tree decoration that can be used year after year. Simple to make, yet very effective, this idea can easily be adapted to make Robins or Santas.

YOU WILL NEED

White, black and orange felt
Thin card
Firm black card
Large white wooden bead
Red ribbon
Black felt-tip pen
Needle and thread
Cotton wool
All-purpose glue
Scissors and saucer

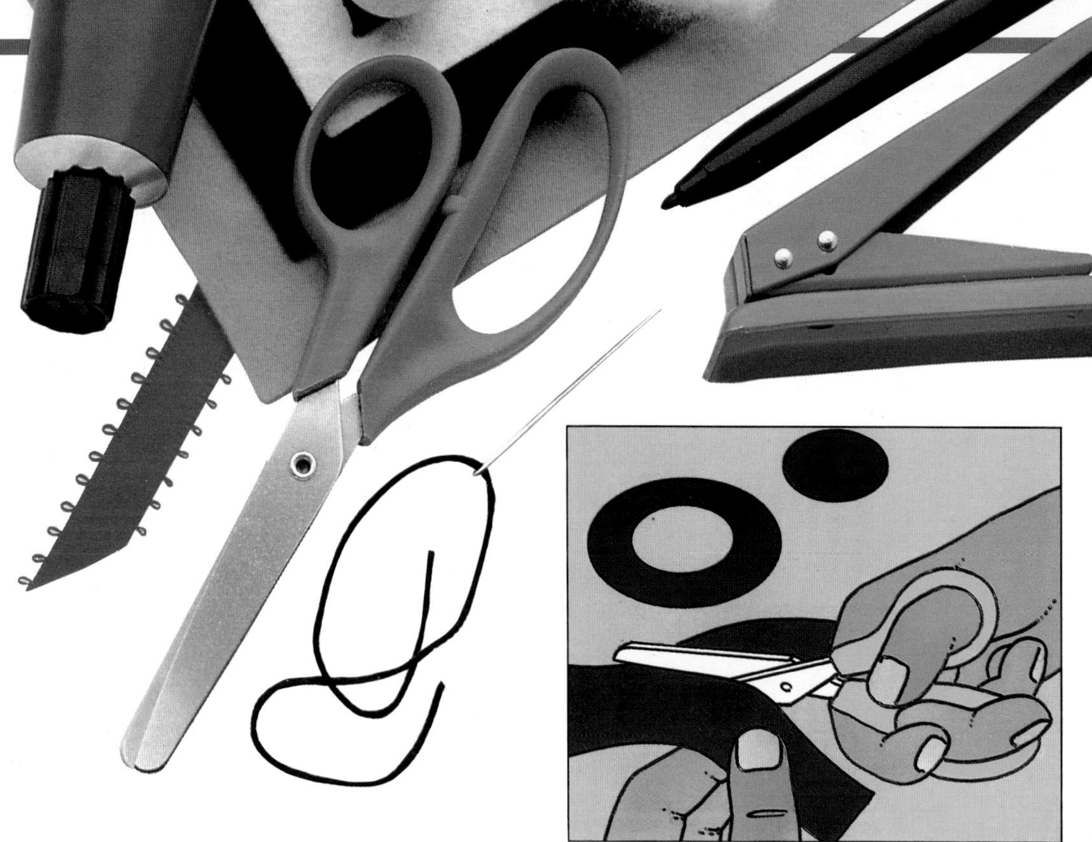

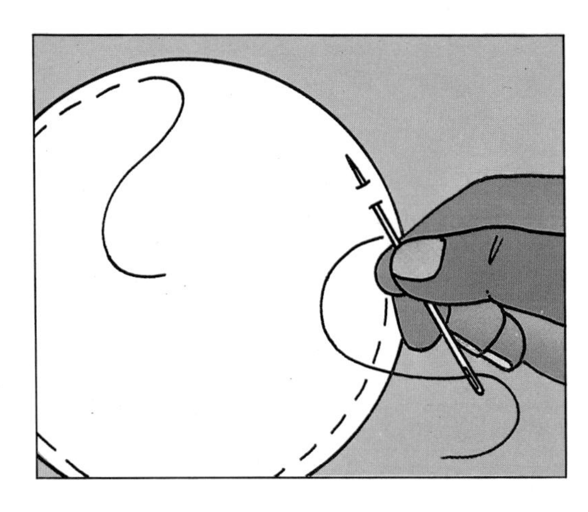

1 Lay a saucer on to some white felt, draw around it with a pen and cut out. Sew around the edge of the circle as shown. Pull the ends of the thread to draw the felt into a ball shape. Leave a gap in the top and the threads hanging.

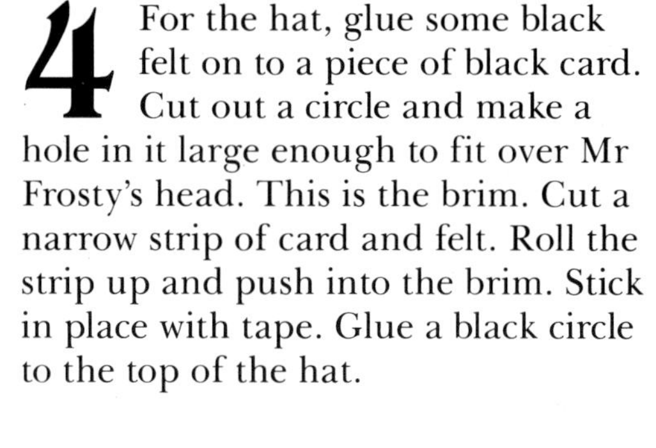

4 For the hat, glue some black felt on to a piece of black card. Cut out a circle and make a hole in it large enough to fit over Mr Frosty's head. This is the brim. Cut a narrow strip of card and felt. Roll the strip up and push into the brim. Stick in place with tape. Glue a black circle to the top of the hat.

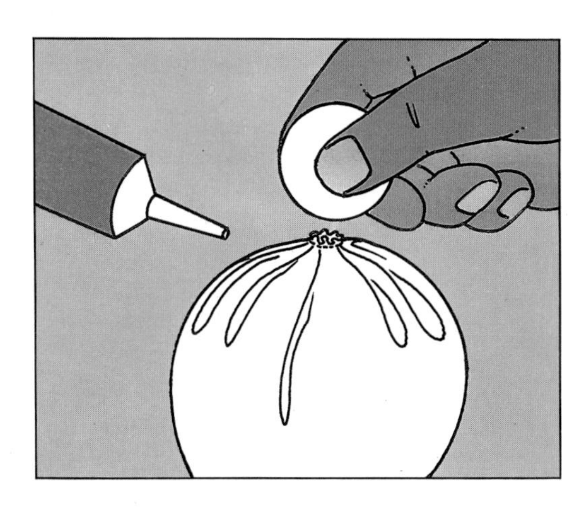

2 Draw a small circle about 4.5cm (1¾in) in diameter on card. Cut out and push into the bottom of the white felt ball. Fill the ball with cotton wool and pull the ends of the thread tightly and knot securely. Glue the wooden bead to the top of the ball.

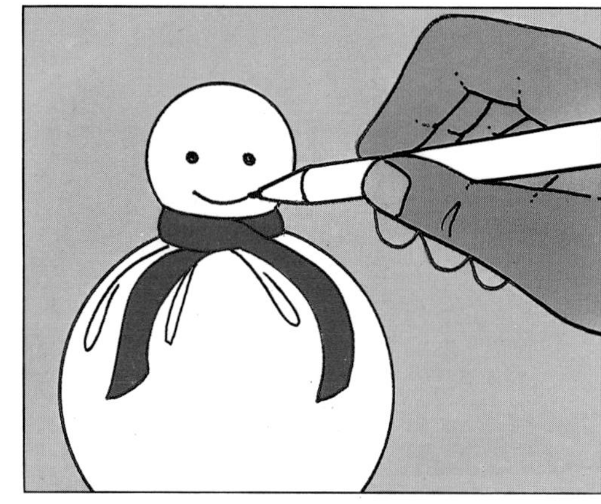

3 Cut a piece of ribbon to make a scarf and glue it in place. Use a black felt-tip pen to draw on Mr Frosty's face and stick on a piece of orange felt for his nose.

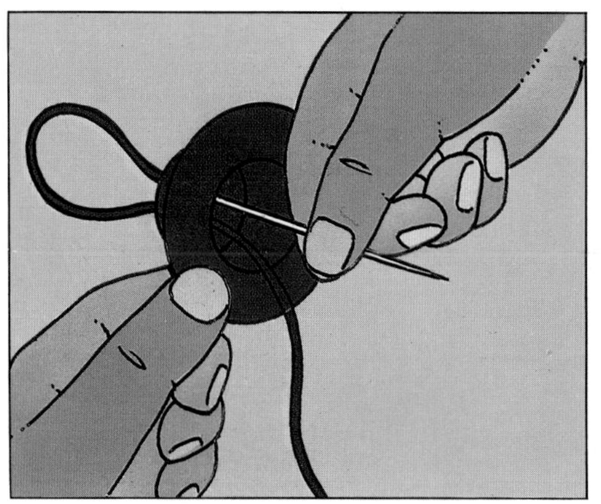

5 Thread a needle with black thread. Push the needle up through the hat and back down again to form a loop. Knot the ends of the thread together inside the hat. Glue the hat to the head.

BELL PENDANT

Empty egg cartons can be cut up to make great bell shapes. Decorate the bell-shaped pieces of carton with shiny foil and tinsel, group them together and make an attractive bell pendant to hang from the wall or ceiling.

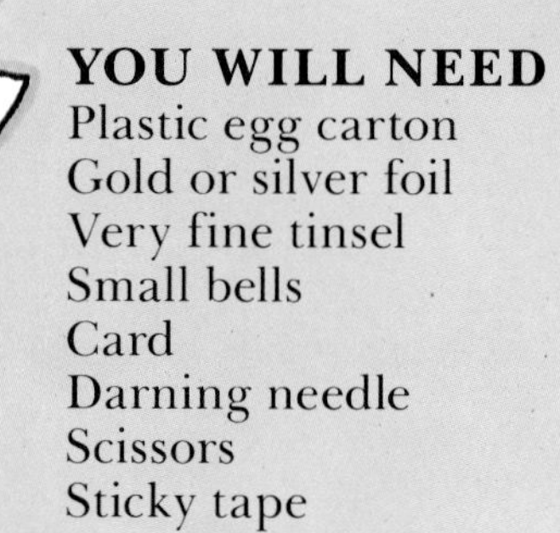

YOU WILL NEED

Plastic egg carton
Gold or silver foil
Very fine tinsel
Small bells
Card
Darning needle
Scissors
Sticky tape

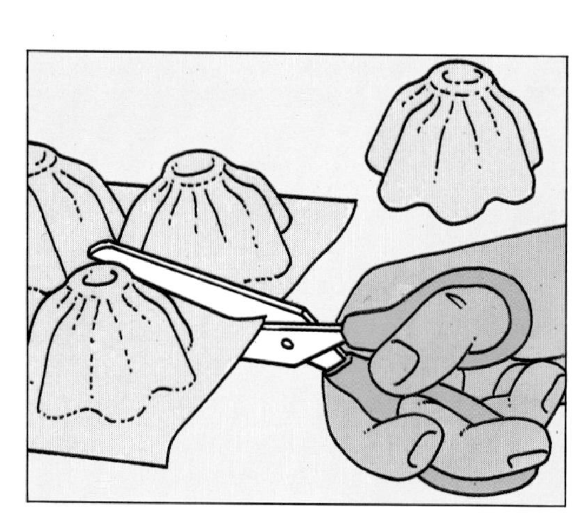

1 Carefully cut out the raised sections of the egg carton using scissors.

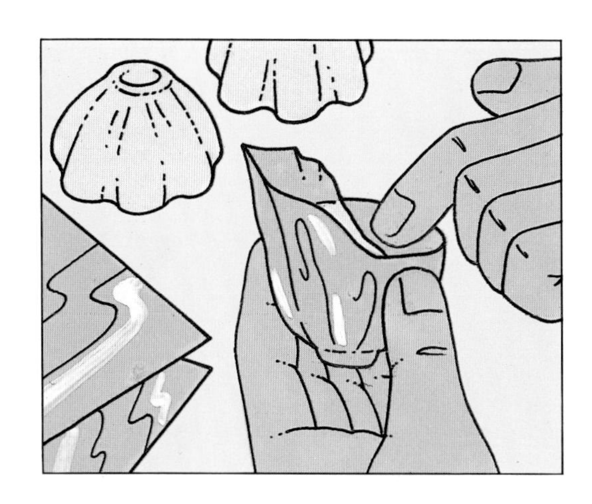

2 Cover the carton pieces with gold or silver foil. Make sure you smooth the foil over the surface and tuck the ends inside the shapes to secure them. If necessary, hold any loose edges in place with tape (not glue) on the inside.

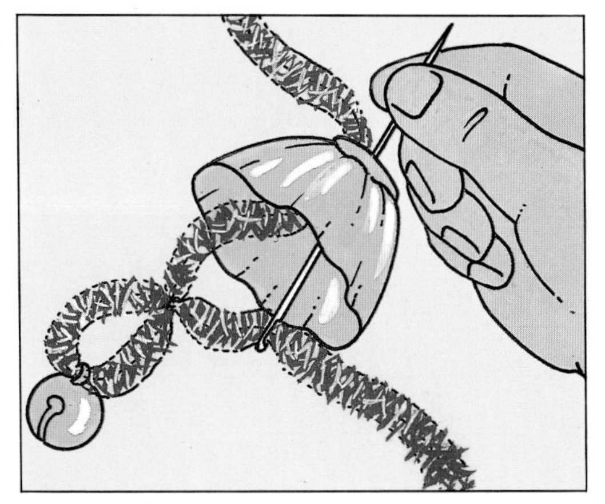

3 Thread the needle with tinsel. Push the needle down through the top of the carton, taking care not to tear the foil. Thread the small bell on to the tinsel. Now take the tinsel back up through the hole in the top of the carton. Knot the pieces of tinsel together inside the carton, about 2.5cm (1in) above the bell. Repeat to make three bell shapes.

4 To make the ring, draw two circles, one inside the other, on to card. Cut the ring out and wrap tinsel around it as you would to make pompons.

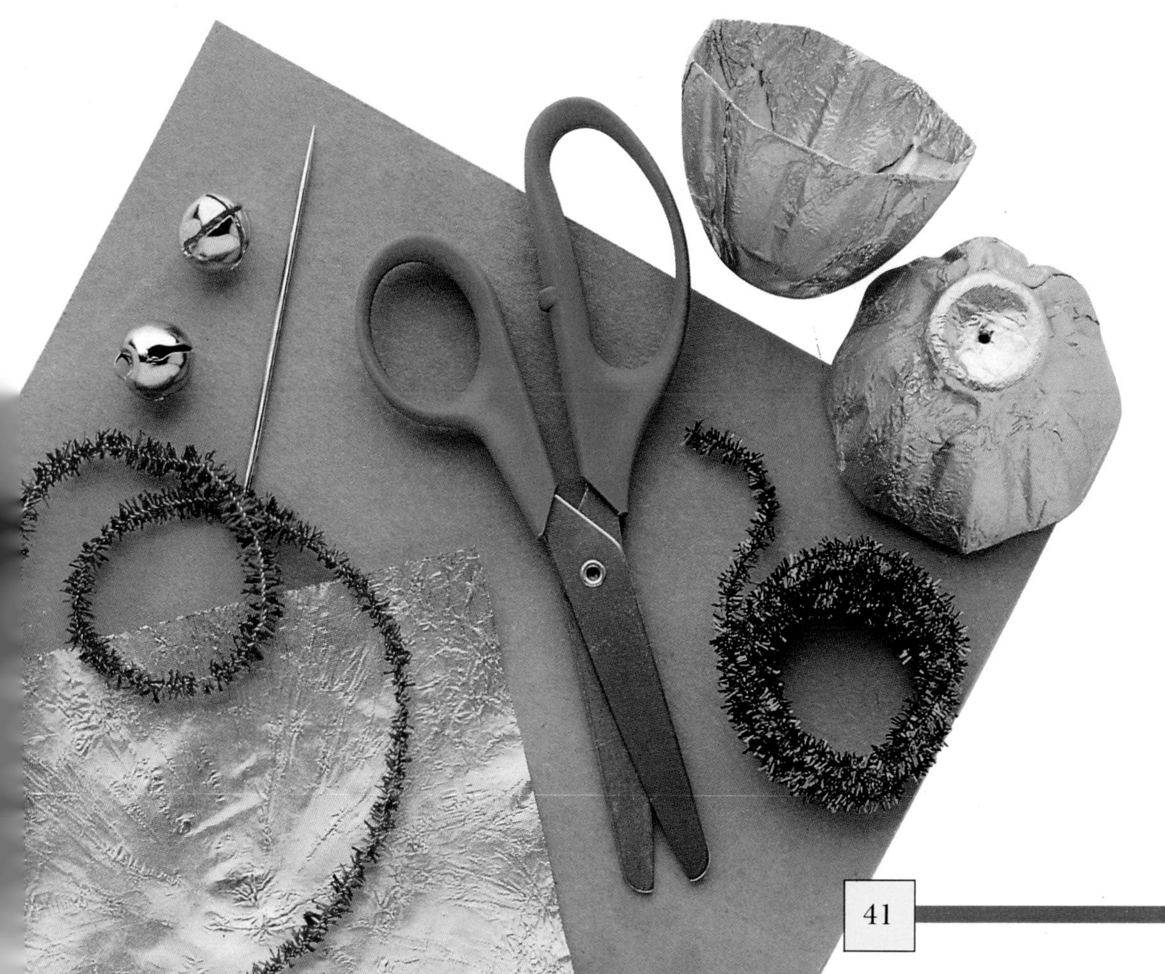

5 Hang the bells on the ring by threading the hanging tinsel through the layers wrapped round the ring. Make sure each bell hangs from a slightly different length. Cut off any loose ends.

CHRISTMAS ANGEL

Put this enchanting angel on the top of your Christmas tree, as a very special decoration. Her skirt is made from soft pink feathers, but you could give her a white feather skirt if you prefer.

YOU WILL NEED

- 1m (1yd) marabou feather trim
- White and gold card
- 5cm (2in) white bead
- All-purpose glue
- Poster paints and paintbrush
- Curling gold paper ribbon
- A pipe cleaner
- 2 gold doilies
- Wooden skewer
- Cotton wool and ribbon
- Masking tape and scissors

1 Trace the cone and hand patterns on page 91. Turn the tracings over and lay on to white card. Rub over the outlines with a pencil. The patterns will appear on the card; cut out. Now cut out a second hand shape. Punch holes into the cone for the arms (see pattern). Roll the cone into shape and tape the join.

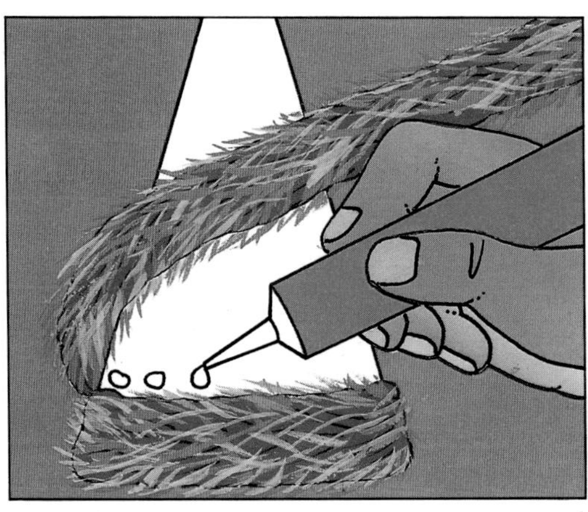

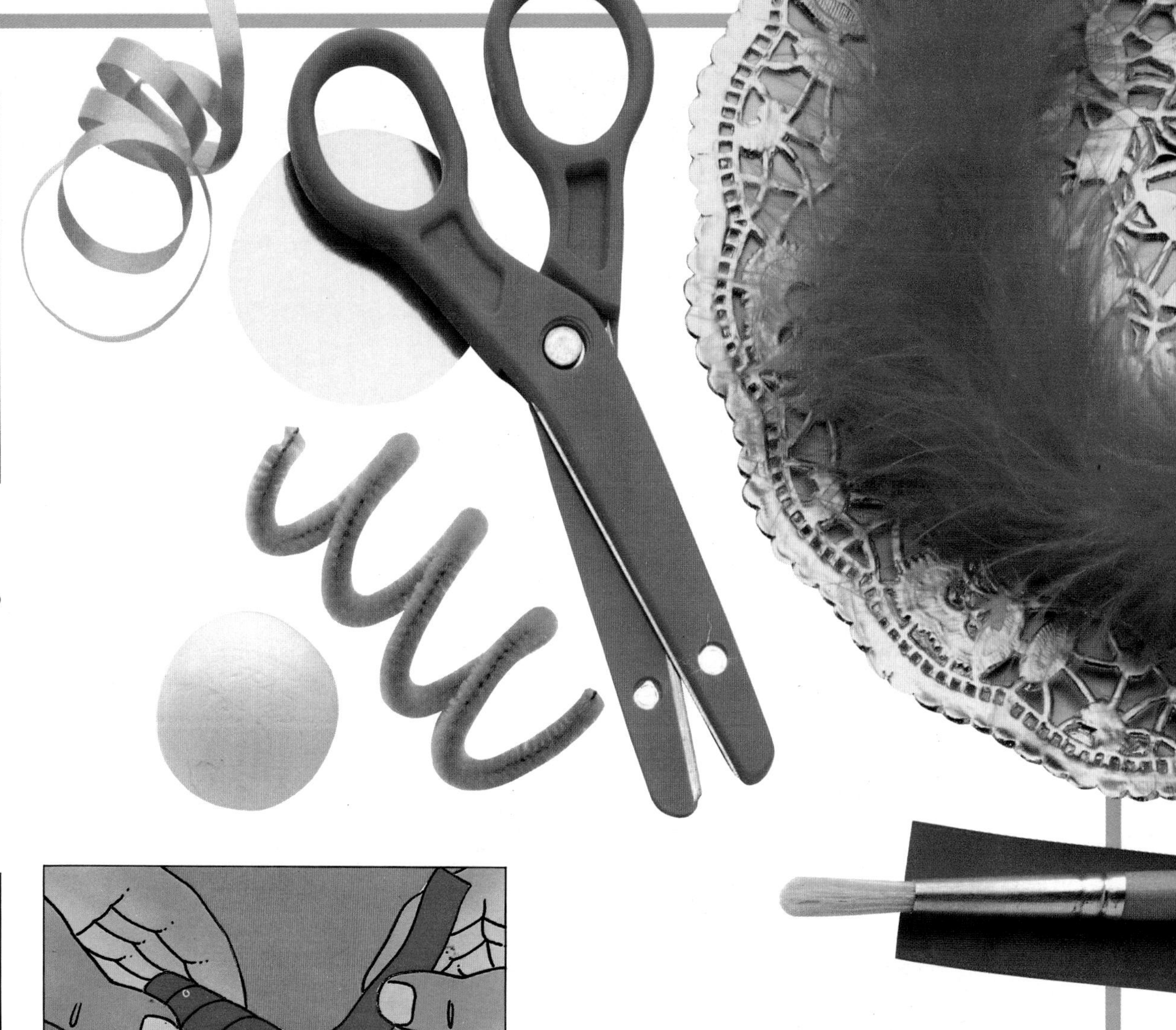

2 Starting at the bottom, wrap the feather trim around the cone. Use small dabs of glue to hold it in place. To make the collar, cut a section from one of the doilies and glue it around the top of the cone.

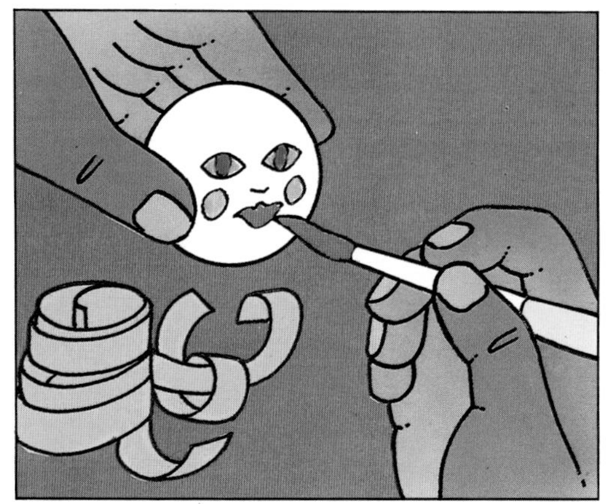

3 Paint a face on the bead. Dribble some glue into the hole in the bead and push in the skewer. Glue lengths of curling ribbon on to the bead for hair.

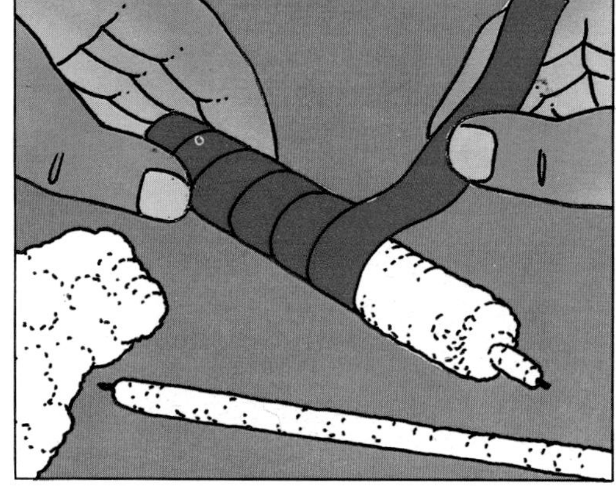

4 To make the arms, cut a pipe cleaner into two 7.5cm (3in) lengths. Glue cotton wool around each one. Leave 6mm (¼in) at each end uncovered. Wrap ribbon over the cotton wool and keep in place with a dab of glue. Glue on the white card hands.

5 Push the arms into the holes in the cone. Push the head into the cone. From the gold card, cut a small square for the book and a circle for the halo. Fold the book in half and glue the hands to each side of it. Fold the doily in half and glue to the angel for wings.

STENCILLED GLITTER CARDS

This form of stencilling uses glitter and glue to make the shapes instead of paint. The stencil is cut from firm paper and can be used again and again to print lots of cards or gift tags.

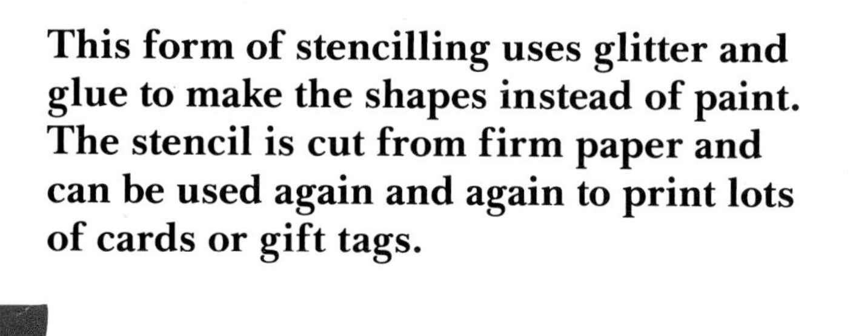

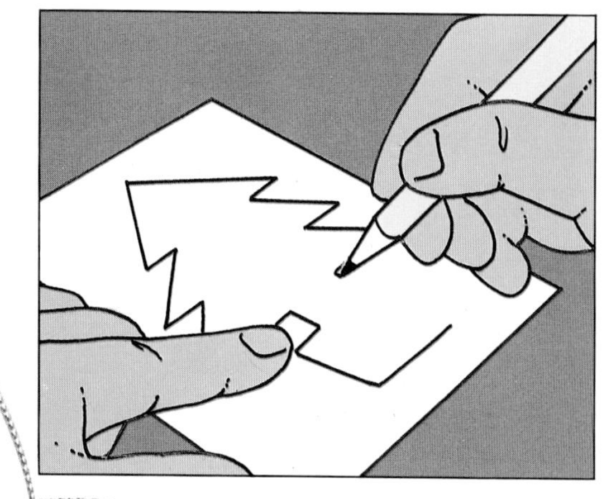

1 Draw your designs on to the firm paper. Objects with strong outlines, like candles, bells and Christmas trees, work well.

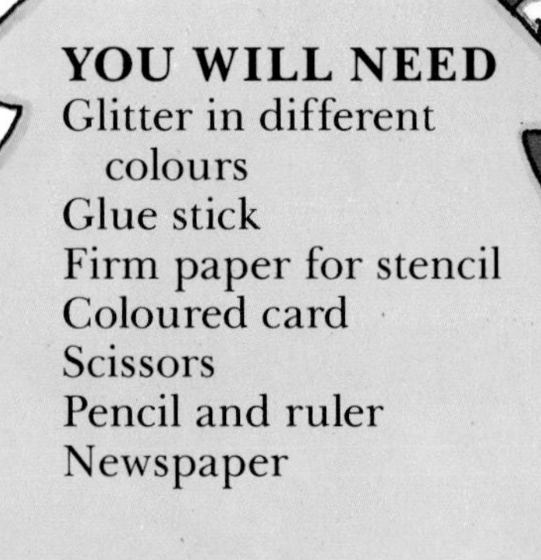

YOU WILL NEED
- Glitter in different colours
- Glue stick
- Firm paper for stencil
- Coloured card
- Scissors
- Pencil and ruler
- Newspaper

2 Push the scissor points into the centre of your design, as shown. Carefully cut out the shape to make a 'window' in the paper. This is the stencil.

3 Cut the card into a rectangle. Place the stencil on top of the card and, holding it firmly in place, apply the glue to the card through the cut-out shape.

4 When all the cut-out area has been completely covered with glue, carefully lift off the stencil. While the glue is still wet, sprinkle the glitter on to it. Leave to dry.

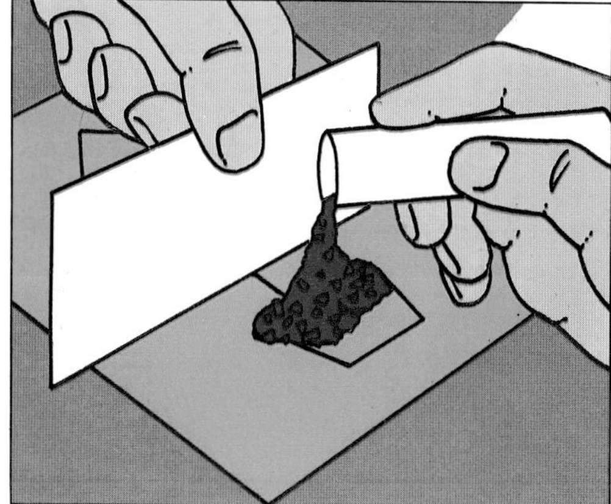

5 To make the glitter stripes, hold the straight edge of a spare piece of card over some of the glued surface, then shake on the glitter. Move the card and apply another colour of glitter. Do this until the shape is covered. To finish, punch a hole through one corner of the card and thread some ribbon through it.

POMPON GARLAND

Pompons are usually made to trim winter hats and outfits – yet if they are made with glittery wool they can be turned into decorations to hang on to the tree, or roped into a pretty garland.

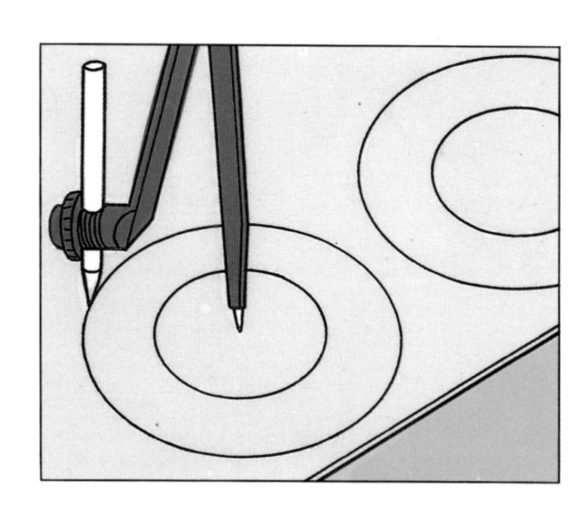

1 Using a compass, draw two circles with a diameter of 4cm (1¼in) on the card. Draw a larger circle about 6½cm (2½in) in diameter around both of the small circles. Cut around the inner and outer circles to give two card rings.

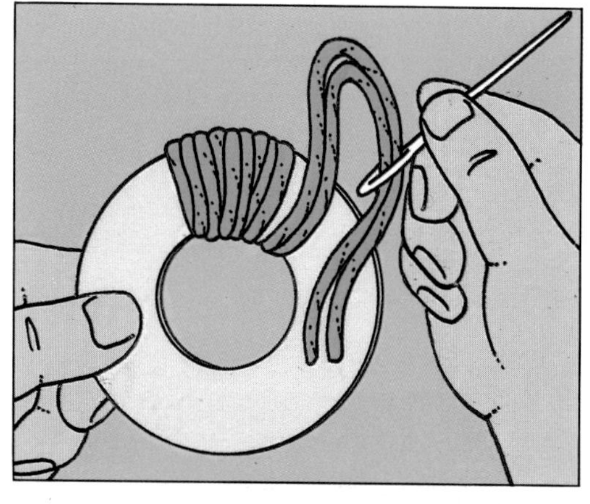

2 Thread the needle with a long length of glittery and standard wool. Bring the ends of the wool together so that you are working with a double thickness of both wools. Take the wool around and around the rings until they are completely covered – you will need to thread the needle a few times.

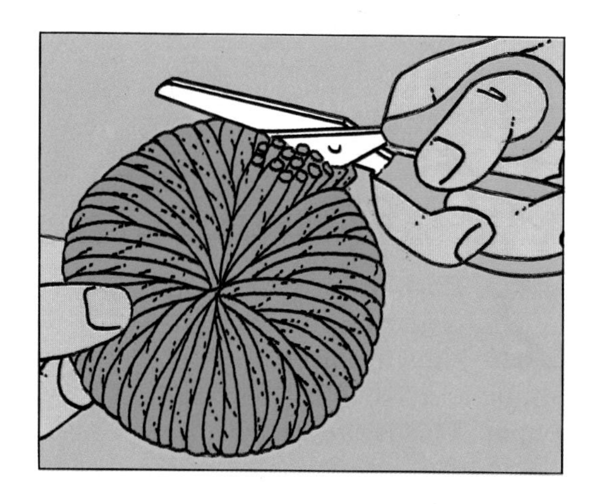

3 When the card is completely covered, slip the blade of the scissors between the two layers of card and cut the wool around the outer edges, as shown.

4 Cut another length of wool and slip it between the two layers of card. Pull it tight and wrap it around the middle of the pompon a few times. Tie it in a firm knot. Slip the card off the pompon and fluff up the wool.

5 For the garland, make lots of pompons and tie them to a thick plait of wool. Use the loose ends of the ties from the centre of the pompon to do this. Individual pompons can be used as ornaments – stitch on a piece of contrasting cord as a loop and hide the join with a bow.

YOU WILL NEED

Glittery and plain wool
Card and a compass
Pencil
Scissors
Ribbons and cord for trims
Darning needle

MINI CARD WREATHS

Decorate your Christmas tree this year with these little wreaths, made from card, ribbons and glittery sequins. The designs shown here are just a guide. You could also try decorating the wreaths with dried flowers, holly leaves and berries.

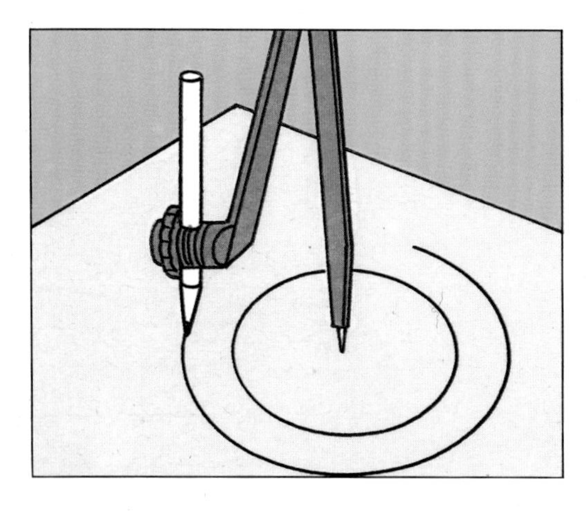

1 Using the compass, draw a circle about 6.5cm (2½ in) in diameter on the card. Leaving the point of the compass in the same position, draw a second circle about 4cm (1½ in) larger than the first. Carefully cut out the wreath.

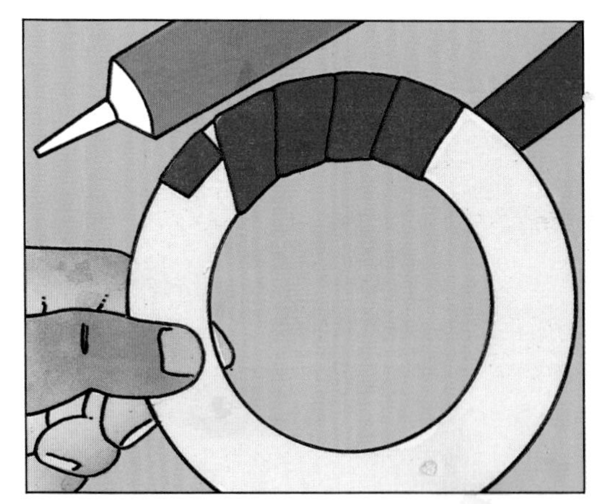

2 Dab some glue on the end of the ribbon and press it to the back of the wreath. When it has dried, twist the ribbon around and around the wreath, so that all the card is covered. Glue the end of the ribbon to the back of the wreath.

3 Repeat with another trim, like sequin strips, this time forming it in much bigger loops. You may like to glue individual sequins on as well. Make a small bow from another coloured ribbon and glue it to the top of the wreath.

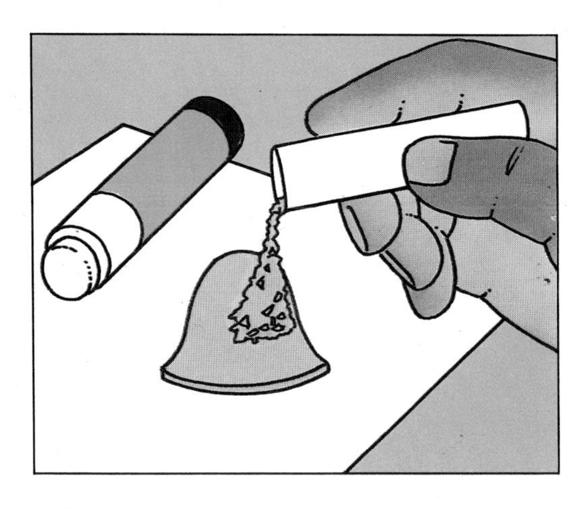

4 Cut out a bell shape from the gold card and lay it on spare paper. Cover the bell with glue and, while still wet, sprinkle glitter on top. Leave it to dry.

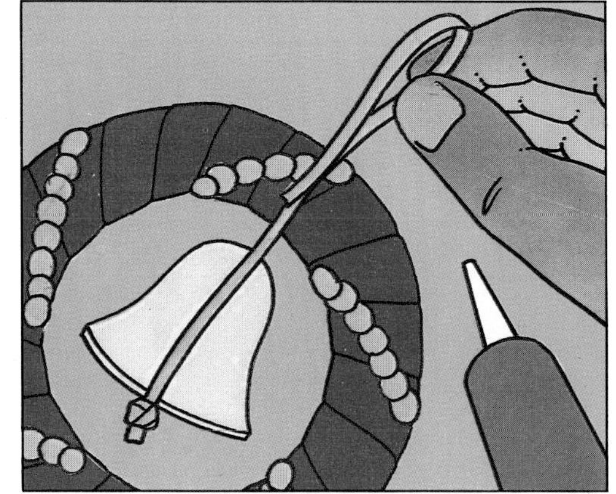

5 Cut a piece of cord about 15cm (6in) long and tie a knot at one end. Glue the back of the bell to the end of the cord. Position the bell in the centre of the wreath, taking the cord up at the back. Fold the cord back down into a loop and glue it behind the wreath.

YOU WILL NEED

Card
Compass
Glitter
All-purpose glue
Scraps of gold card
Ribbons, cords and sequins
Pencil
Scissors

RIBBON ROSETTES

These ribbon rosettes are very quick and easy to make yet give a really stylish finish to your Christmas presents. Try tying your parcels with shiny, metallic ribbon and making a matching rosette for the top.

1 Cut eight lengths of ribbon 20cm (8in) long. Cut a small piece of ribbon 5cm (2in) long, for the central loop.

4 To make a two-colour bow, cut four pieces each of two different coloured ribbons. Make eight bow loops as in step 2. Criss-cross the loops, using first one colour then another, before finishing with a small centre loop.

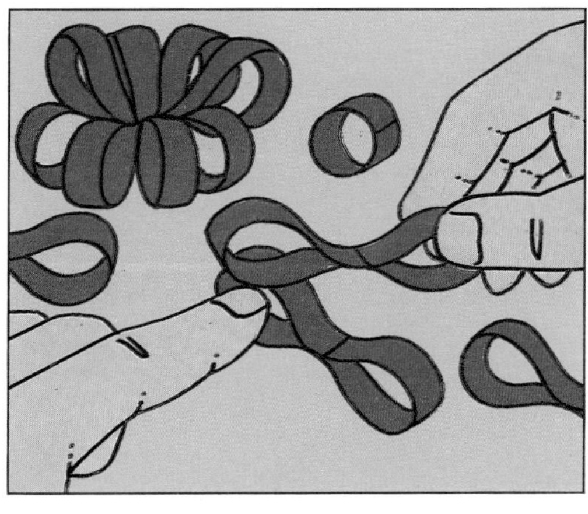

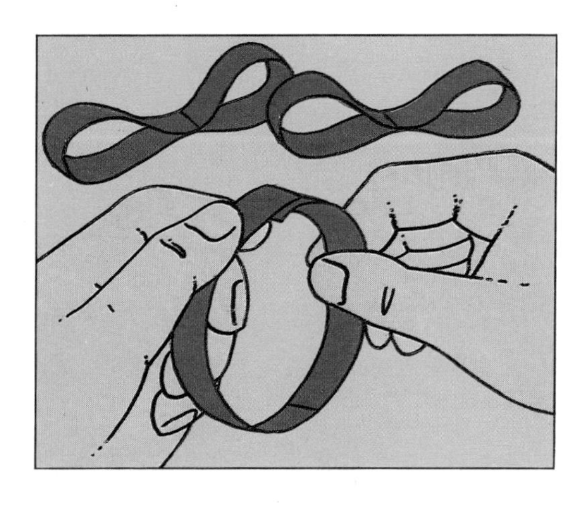

2 Overlap the ends of each of the long lengths of ribbon and stick together with double-sided tape to form a loop. Join each loop in the middle, using tape on the inside of the loop, as shown.

3 Tape the loops together by placing each one diagonally on top of the one below, to form a criss-cross pattern. To finish, tape the ends of the short piece of ribbon together to form a tiny loop. Tape this neatly in the centre of the rosette.

SANTA GLOVE PUPPET

Make this smiling Santa glove puppet to give away as a Christmas present or keep for yourself. You can also try drawing your own patterns to create a whole family of puppet characters.

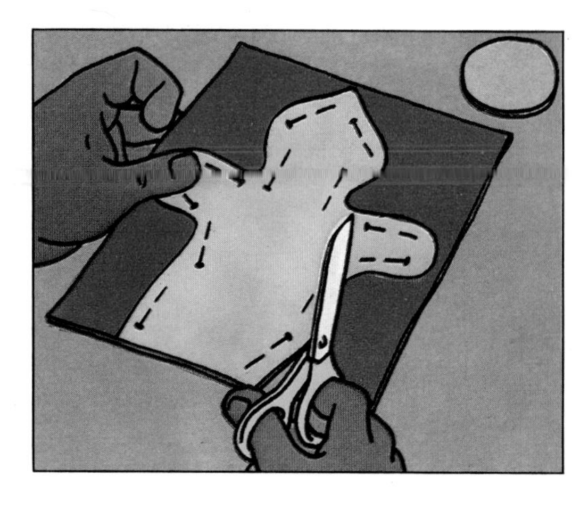

1 Using a pencil, trace the patterns on page 92. You will need three patterns to make the Santa. Trace the body pattern around the solid line, the face pattern around the dotted line and the beard around the broken line. Cut out the three patterns. Pin the body pattern on to red felt, and cut out two shapes.

2 Pin the face pattern on to pink felt and cut out. Glue the face to one puppet. Sew on the red bead nose. Stitch the two body shapes together, leaving the bottom of the puppet open.

YOU WILL NEED

Red, pink and black felt
White fur fabric
A red bead
Red cotton and needle
Fabric glue
Scissors
Tracing paper and pencil
Pins

3 Pin the beard pattern to the back of the fur fabric. Cut out the beard and carefully cut out the mouth as marked. Glue the beard under Santa's nose.

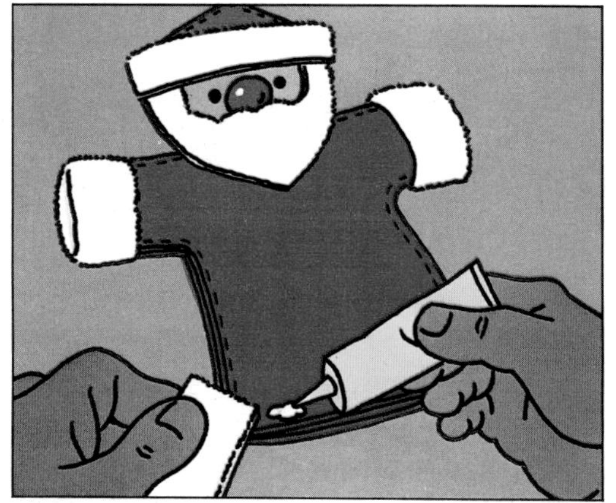

4 Cut out strips of fur fabric to fit around the bottom of the puppet, around each arm and around the head. Glue the strips in place. Cut out two black felt eyes and glue in position on the face. Cut out a fur fabric hat bobble and glue to the top of the hat.

GIFT SOAPS

Make a small present look really special by taking extra time and effort to wrap it. Miniature soaps look lovely wrapped in two layers of brightly coloured net and secured with a pretty bow.

YOU WILL NEED

- Miniature soaps or bath balls
- Net in two colours
- Ribbon
- Scissors
- Two plates – one slightly smaller than the other
- Small rubber bands
- Ball-point pen

1 Take a piece of net in each colour. Lay the large plate on to one piece of net and the smaller plate on to the other. Draw round both plates with a pen and cut out the two circles.

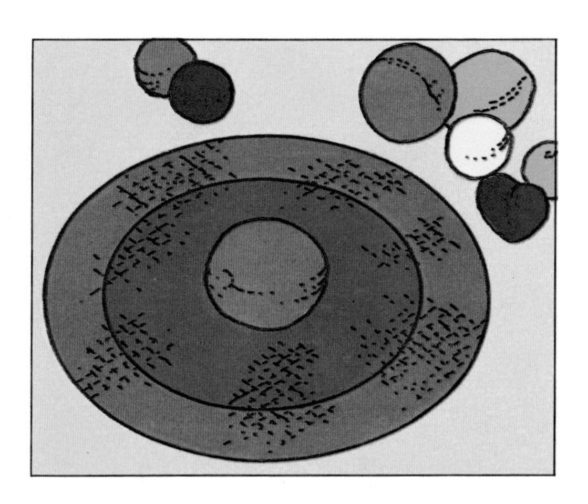

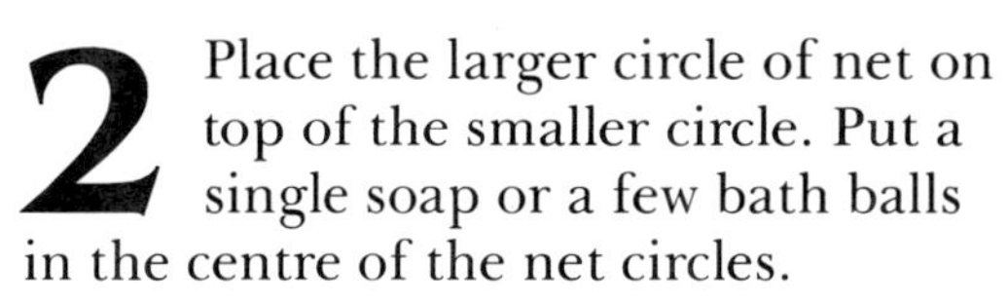

2 Place the larger circle of net on top of the smaller circle. Put a single soap or a few bath balls in the centre of the net circles.

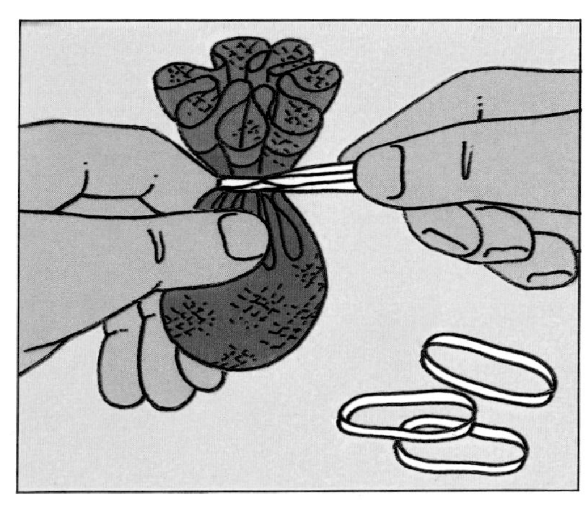

3 Bunch both circles of net up around the soap. Secure in place with a small elastic band. Pull the net about a little to make an attractive frill.

4 Decorate the soap bags with a matching ribbon, making sure you cover the rubber band. Tie into a bow at the front.

HANDMADE GIFTWRAP

This Christmas, wrap up your presents in paper that you have printed. Any lightweight paper can be used and the prints are made from festive shapes cut out of household sponges.

YOU WILL NEED

Sponge cloths
Poster paints and paintbrush
Card
Glue and pen
Scissors
Paper to print

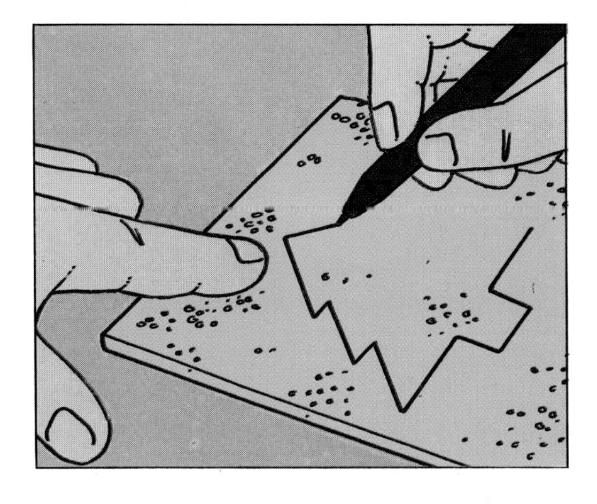

1 Plan your designs on scrap paper first. Shapes with strong outlines work best. Draw the shapes on to the sponge cloth and cut them out with scissors.

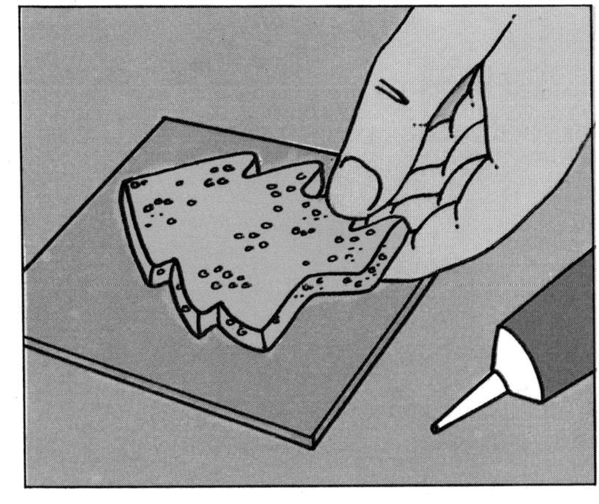

2 Cut a piece of card slightly larger than the sponge shape and stick the shape on to it. This makes it easier to print without getting paint on your hands.

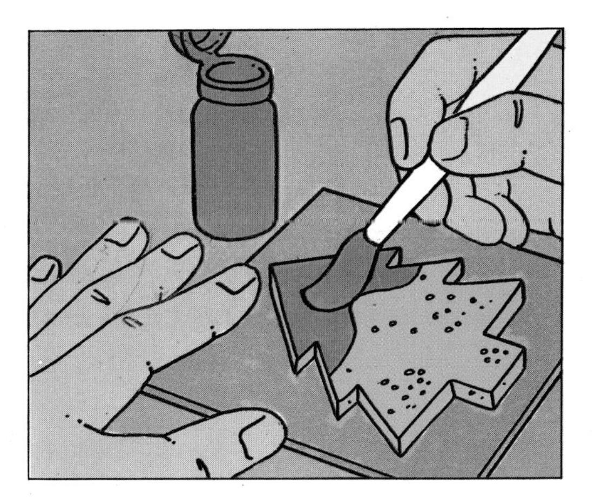

3 Lay the paper to be printed on a flat surface. Use the paint straight from the pot and, with the brush, cover the surface of the sponge shape with paint.

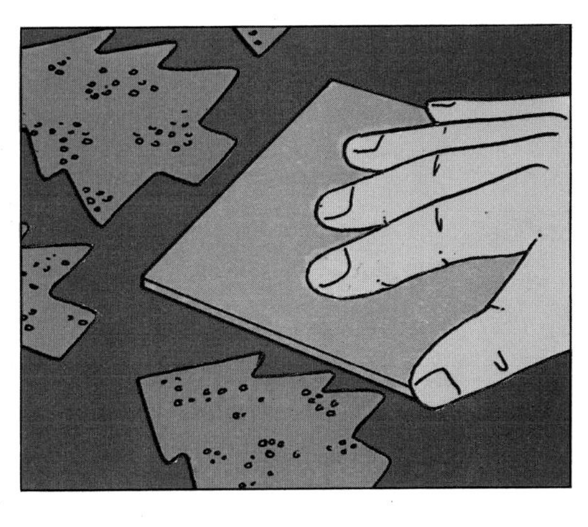

4 Holding the edges of the card, gently press the sponge on to the paper, then lift it off. Press it down again on another spot. When the colour gets too faint, coat the sponge with more paint. Use a new sponge shape if you want to print other colours.

STARS AND BELLS

These bright and shiny stars and bells are easy to make and will look very pretty hanging from your Christmas tree. You can also make a colourful garland by stringing the decorations on to ribbon.

YOU WILL NEED
Shiny cardboard
Star stickers
Shiny giftwrap ribbon
Hole punch
Scissors
Tracing paper and pencil

1 Using a pencil, trace the patterns on page 93. Cut out the patterns and hold in position on the back of the shiny cardboard. Draw around the patterns and cut out the shapes.

2 To make more stars and bells, lay the shapes you have just cut out on to card and draw around them. Cut out as many shapes as you like.

3 Punch a hole in your decorations so you will be able to hang them up. Decorate them with gold and silver stickers.

4 Thread ribbon through the holes you have made. To make a garland, thread lots of stars and bells on to ribbon.

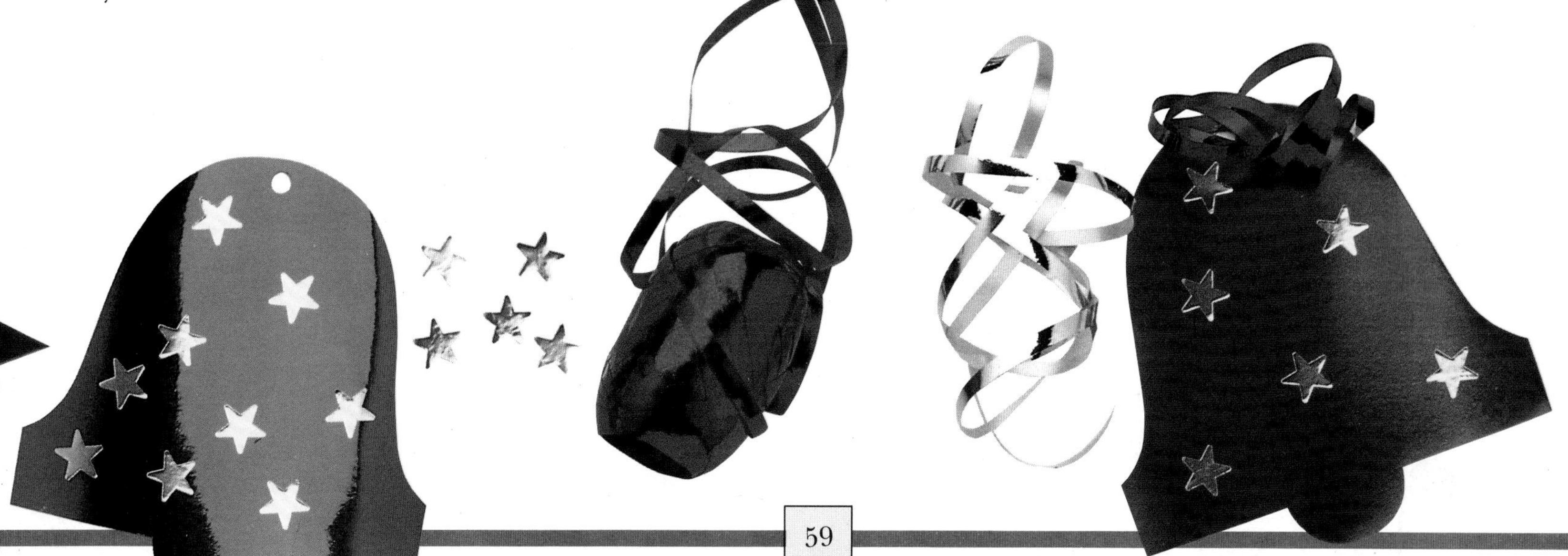

REINDEER HAT

Give everyone a smile at Christmas with this jolly reindeer party hat. Make your hat as glamorous as you can by adding lots of shiny ribbon, glitter and beads.

YOU WILL NEED

Green and beige card
3 yellow pipe cleaners
Wooden bead
Red glitter
Black felt-tip pen
2 bells
Giftwrapping ribbon
Strings of beads
All-purpose glue
Tracing paper and pencil
Scissors

1 Cut a strip of green card 8cm (3¼in) wide and long enough to go round your head. Overlap the ends and glue together. Glue giftwrapping ribbon and beads in loops around the hat.

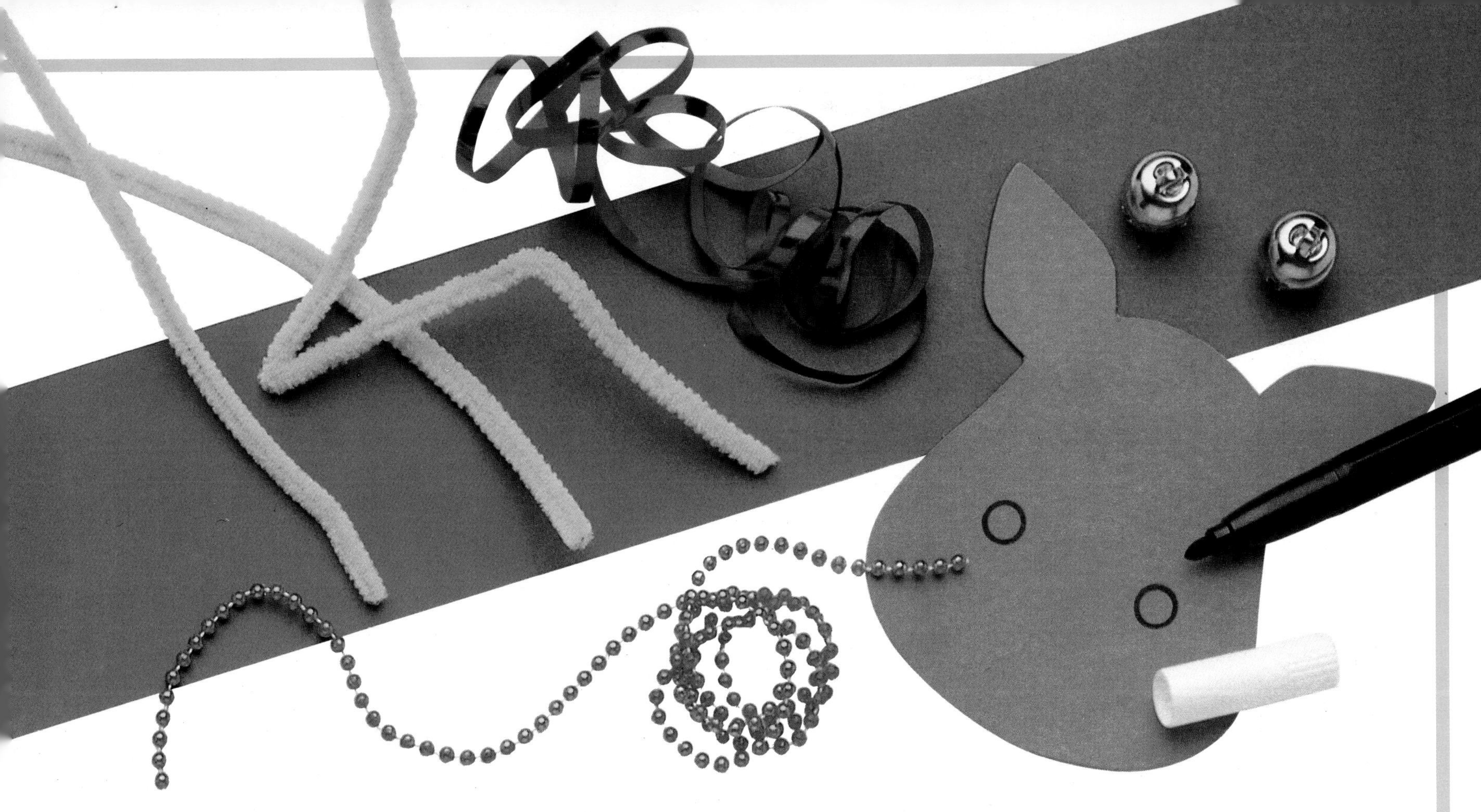

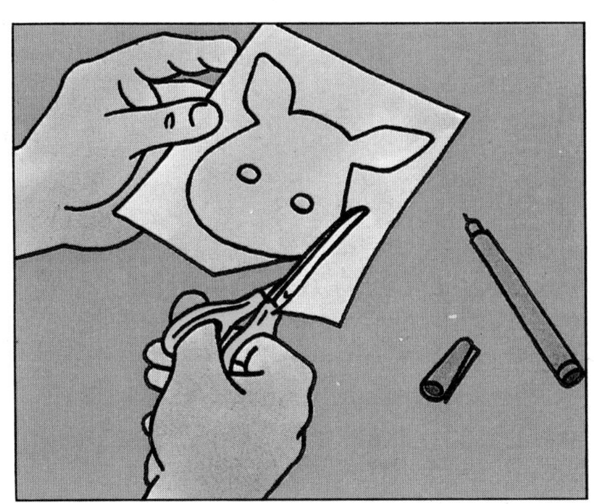

2 Using a pencil, trace the reindeer face on page 94. Turn the tracing paper over and lay it on the beige card. Rub firmly over the outline with a pencil. The image will appear on the card. Cut out the face. Draw the eyes with a felt-tip pen.

3 Cover the bead with glue and sprinkle it with glitter. Leave to dry and then glue it to the reindeer's face. To make the antlers, bend the pipe cleaners in half and glue them behind the head, as shown.

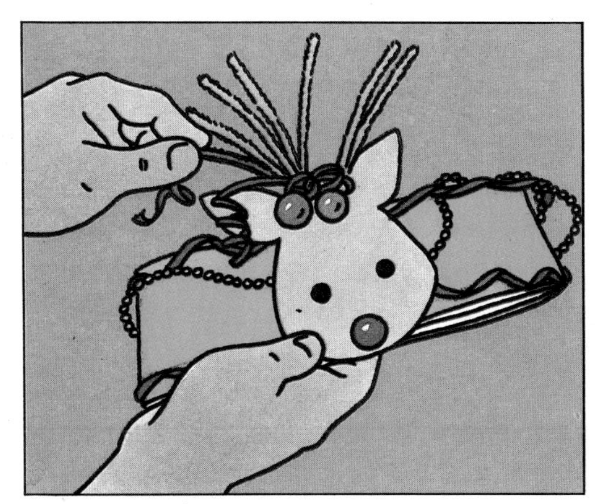

4 Glue the reindeer face to the green card strip. Tie the bells on to some ribbon and tie these around the antlers so that they rest between the reindeer's ears. Bend the pipe cleaners over slightly to give the antlers some shape.

FESTIVE JEWELLERY

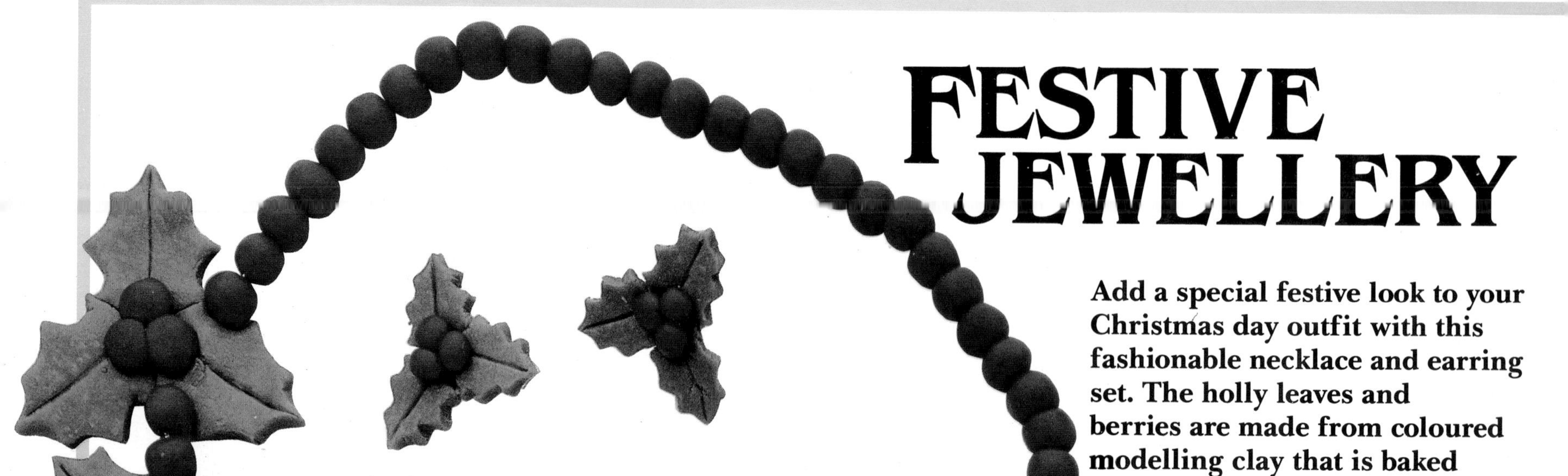

Add a special festive look to your Christmas day outfit with this fashionable necklace and earring set. The holly leaves and berries are made from coloured modelling clay that is baked in the oven.

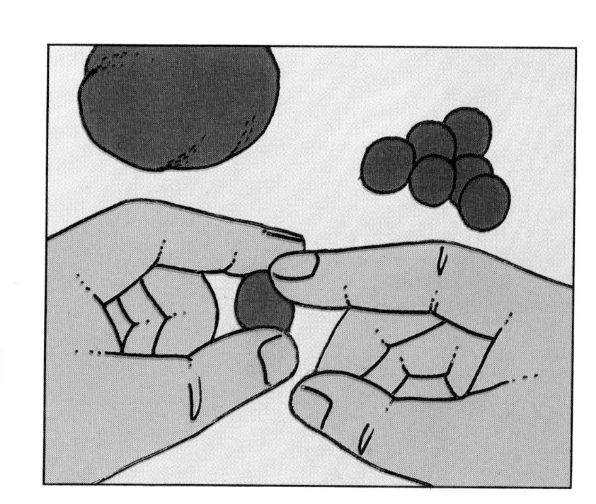

3 Roll some red modelling clay in your hands to make small balls to use as berries for the necklace and the earrings.

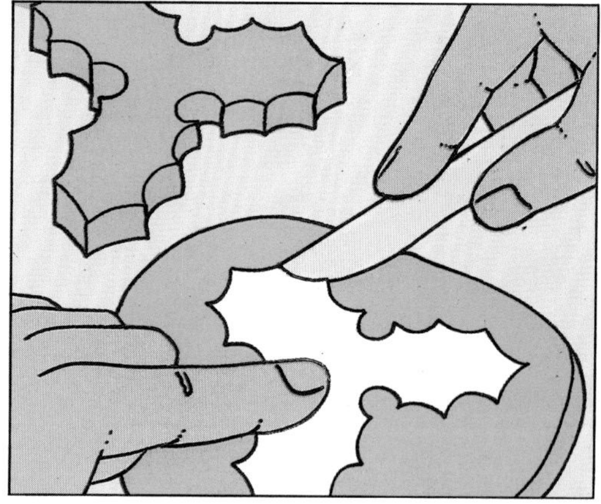

2 Roll out some green modelling clay on to a smooth surface. Press the holly pattern into the clay and cut around it. Cut out three clusters of leaves.

1 Draw a cluster of three holly leaves on to some card. Cut the shape out and use it as a pattern for your jewellery.

SAFETY TIP: *Make sure an adult helps you when using the oven.*

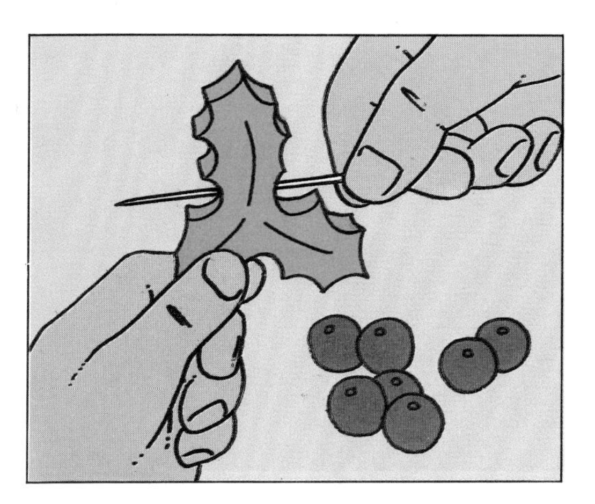

4 To make the necklace, carefully push the darning needle through one leaf from one edge to the other. Press three berries into the centre of the cluster. Push the darning needle through the centre of the remaining berries. For the earrings, draw a small cluster of holly leaves on to card and cut two earring shapes from clay. Decorate with berries.

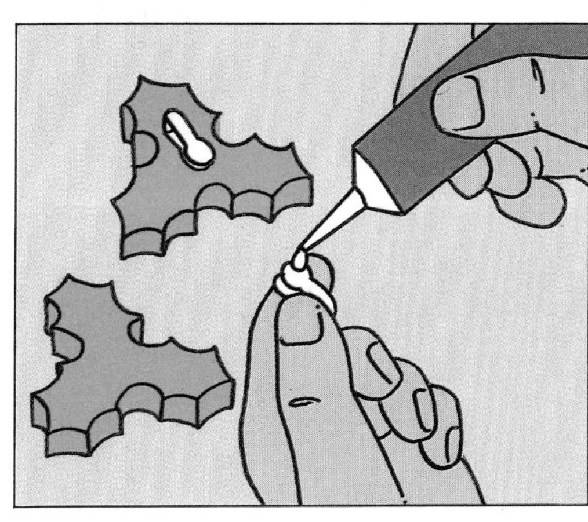

5 Bake the shapes in the oven following the instructions on the packet. Wearing oven gloves, remove the shapes from the oven and leave to cool before making up the jewellery. For the necklace, thread the berries and the leaves onto the braid and knot the ends. For the earrings, glue clip-on earring backs to the back of the leaves.

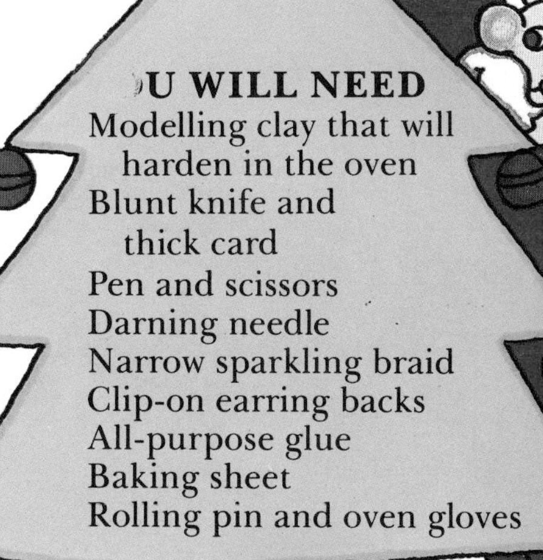

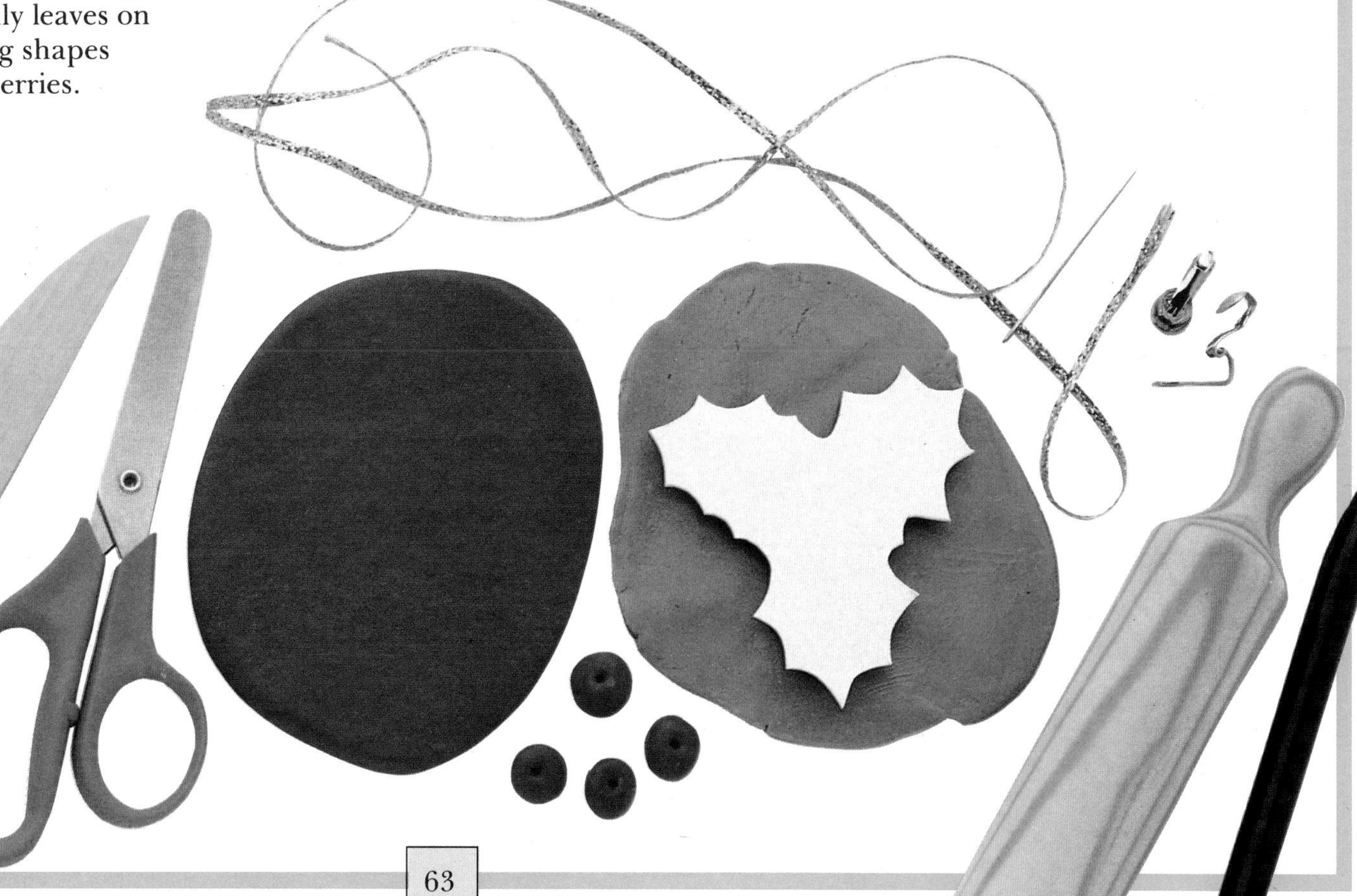

1
2
3
4
5
6
7
8
9
10
11
12
13
14
15
16
17
18
19
20
21
22
23
24

ADVENT CALENDAR

Advent calendars are designed to contain a message or a small gift, which you open on each of the 24 days leading up to Christmas – so you will need to make this calendar well in advance. To celebrate Christmas Eve, you could make the gift inside the last matchbox extra special.

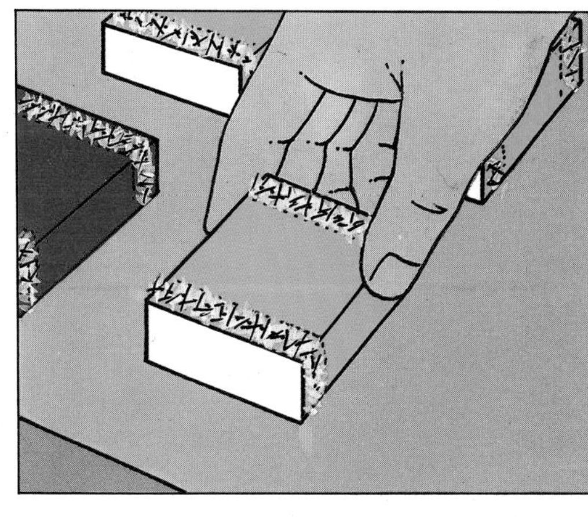

1 Cut the foil into strips the same width as the matchboxes and long enough to wrap around them. Coat the foil with glue and wrap it around the matchbox. Glue tinsel around each end of the matchbox.

2 Position the matchboxes on the gold card, so they are in six rows. Glue them in place. Put some books on top of the matchboxes to weight them. Leave them to dry.

3 Using the glitter pens, draw the numbers 1 to 24 on the boxes. Cut two holly leaves from green foil and berries from red foil, and glue them to the top of the calendar.

4 Glue some paper ribbon around the outer edges of the gold card. Glue a loop of tinsel to the top. Put a sweet or small gift inside each of the boxes.

YOU WILL NEED

- 46cm x 40cm (18½in x 16in) gold mounting board
- 24 empty matchboxes
- Coloured foil paper
- Glitter pens
- Fine tinsel and paper ribbon
- All-purpose glue
- 24 sweets or small gifts

CHRISTMAS CRACKERS

Christmas crackers are a traditional party decoration for the festive season. This year, make your own crackers to hang on the Christmas tree or to add a sparkle to the dinner table. You could also put extra special gifts inside for a seasonal treat.

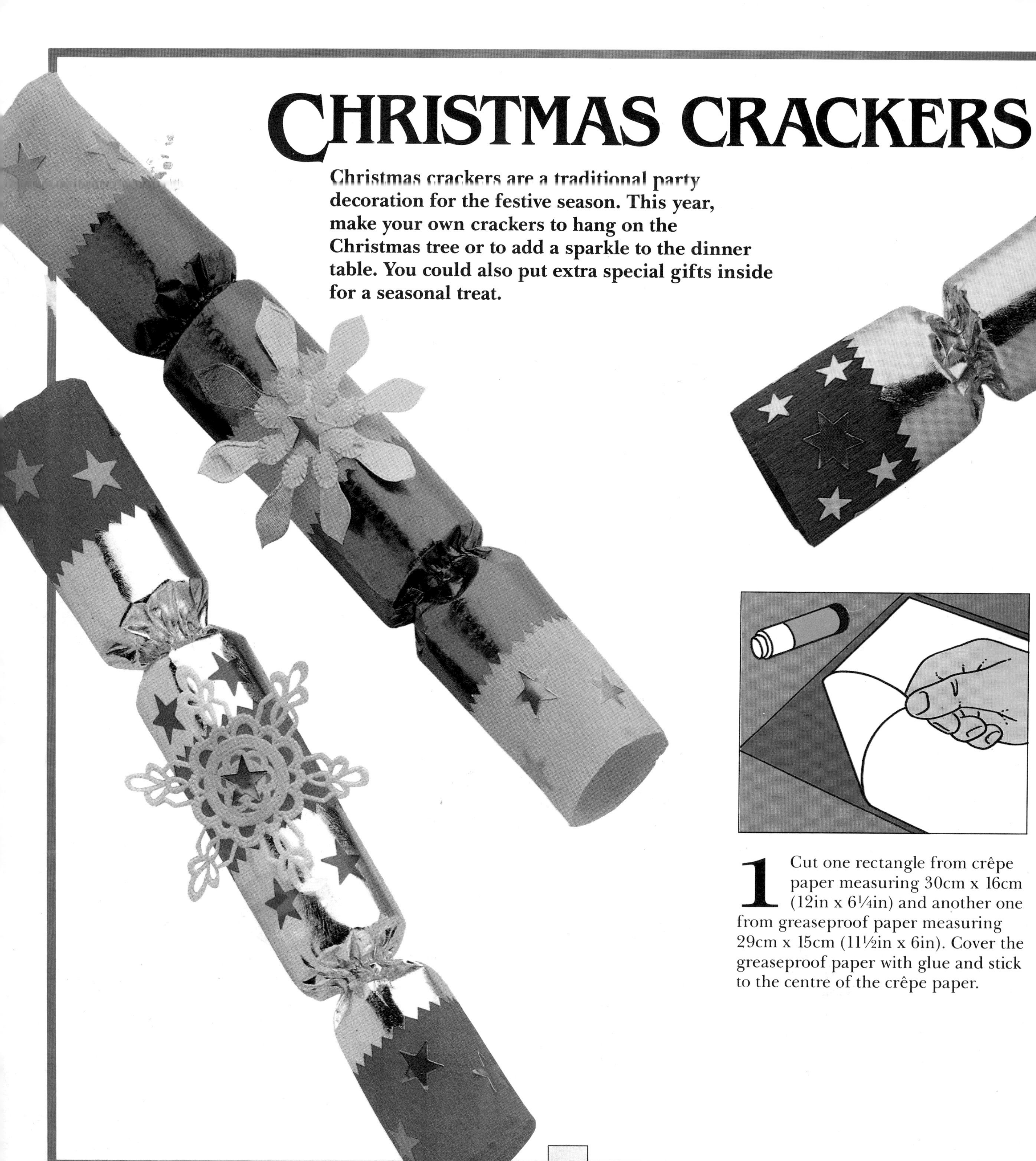

1 Cut one rectangle from crêpe paper measuring 30cm x 16cm (12in x 6¼in) and another one from greaseproof paper measuring 29cm x 15cm (11½in x 6in). Cover the greaseproof paper with glue and stick to the centre of the crêpe paper.

5 Untie the string; the shiny giftwrap should hold its shape. Decorate the cracker with pieces cut from gold and silver doilies and brightly-coloured stick-on stars.

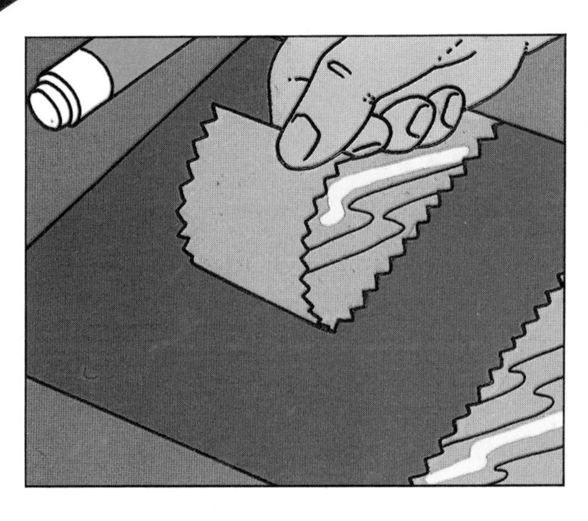

2 Cut two strips of shiny giftwrap 16cm x 9cm ($6\frac{1}{4}$in x $3\frac{1}{2}$in). Snip zigzag lines along the long edges and glue to the crêpe paper as shown.

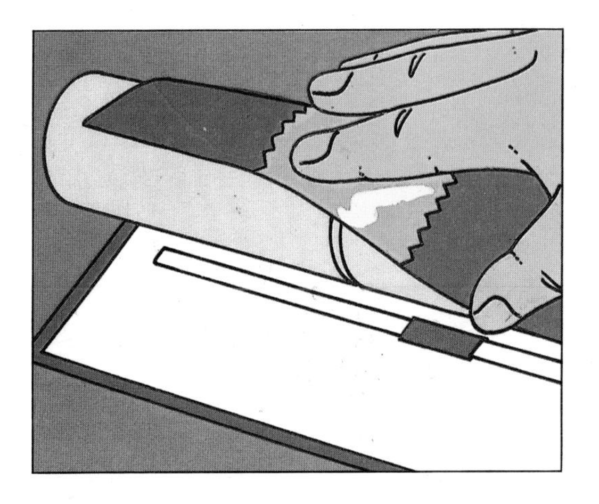

3 Lay the three cardboard tubes in the centre of the greaseproof paper. Add the cracker snap and roll up tightly. Glue the overlapped edges of paper together.

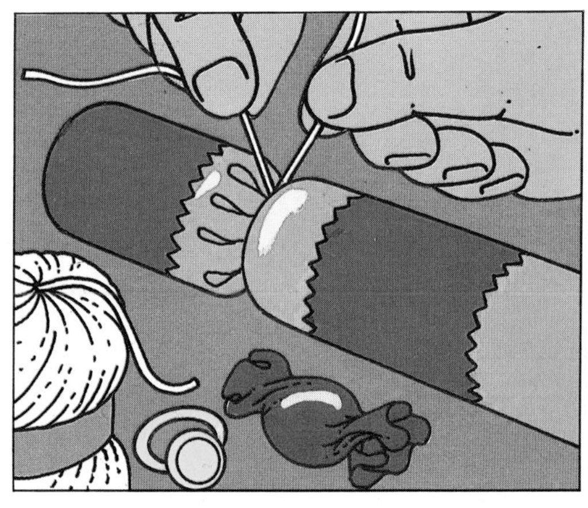

4 Remove the tubes at each end, leaving the centre one in place. Tie a piece of string tightly around one end of the cracker, as shown. Put a gift and a hat into the tube. Tie another piece of string around the other end of the cracker.

ROYAL CROWN

If you have to dress up for a Christmas fancy dress party go as one of the three kings, wearing this fabulous crown. Decorate it with foil sweet wrappers to look like jewels.

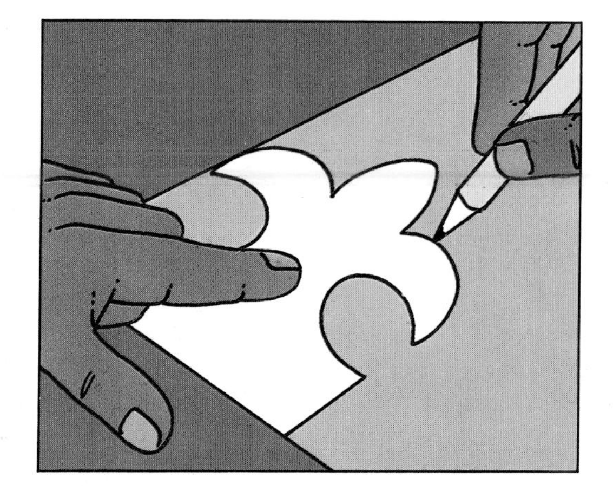

1 Using a pencil, trace the pattern on page 94. Turn the tracing paper over and lay it on a piece of scrap card. Rub firmly over the outline with a pencil. The image will appear on the card. Cut out the pattern. This is one section of the crown. Put the pattern on the gold card so that the straight edges match up. Draw around the shape.

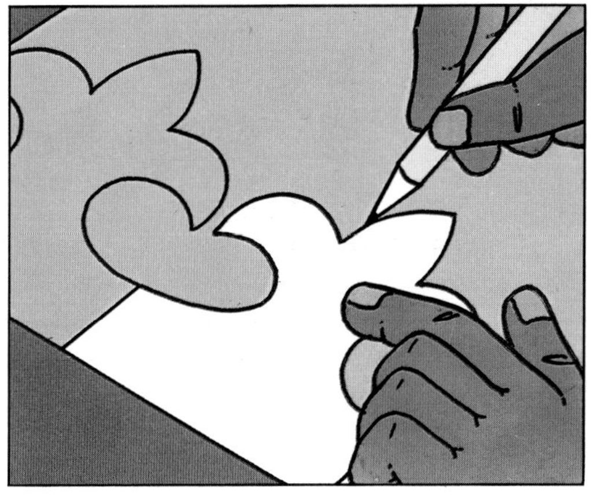

2 Move the pattern along and position it against the shape you have just drawn, as shown. Make sure the short sides match. Draw around the shape again. Repeat this until you have drawn around the pattern five times.

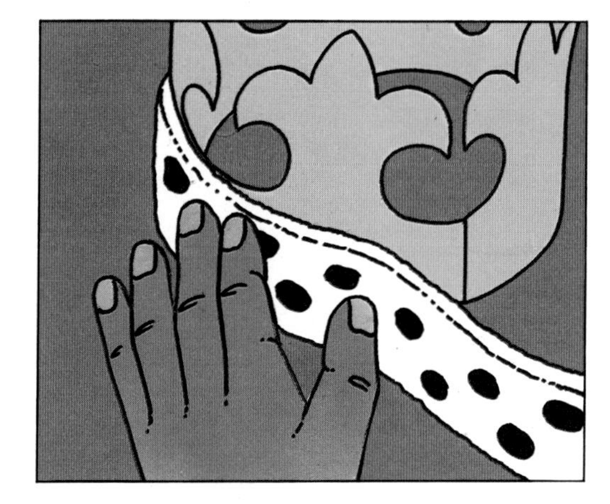

3 Carefully cut out the crown shape. Paint black dashes on the wadding and leave it to dry. Curve the crown into shape, overlapping the edges. Tape the join on the inside. Glue the wadding to the lower edge of the crown, butting the edges together.

4 Cut squares from the coloured foil and glue them on to the crown to look like jewels.

YOU WILL NEED

Lightweight gold card
Coloured foil sweet wrappers
Wadding 65cm x 6cm (26in x 2¼in)
Black paint and paintbrush
Masking tape
Scissors
Scrap card
All-purpose glue
Tracing paper and pencil

TOTE BAGS

Paper tote bags are much easier to make than they look and are great for wrapping awkwardly-shaped Christmas presents. You can line Christmas giftwrap with plain paper to make sturdy tote bags in a variety of sizes. Use white paper for the lining, or a colour to match the giftwrap.

1 To make the lining, cut a piece of plain paper large enough to wrap around two or three books with at least 5cm (2in) extra at the top and bottom.

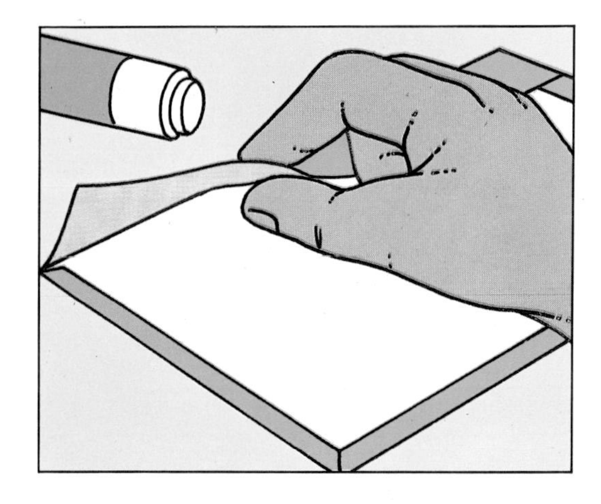

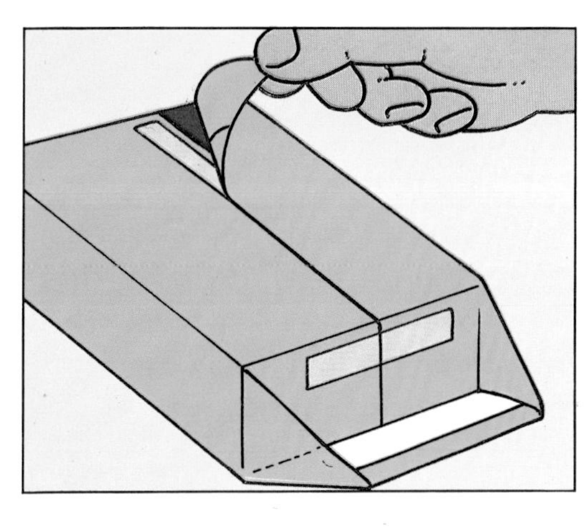

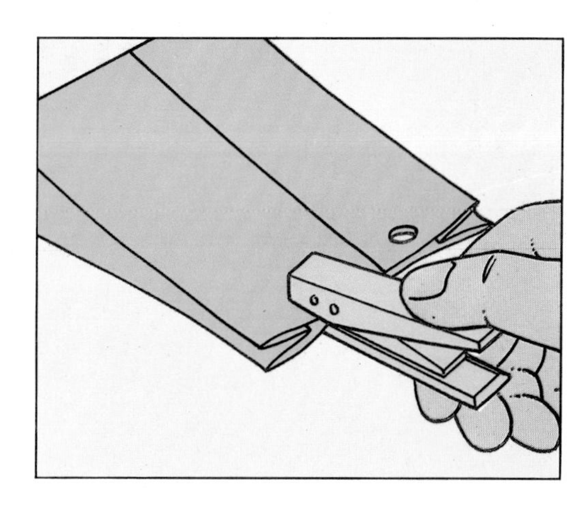

2 Cut a piece of giftwrap 1cm (½in) larger all round than the plain paper. Glue the plain paper to the wrong side of the giftwrap. Fold in the edges of the giftwrap and glue them down. Fold the top edge down again by about 5cm (2in).

3 Wrap the lined giftwrap around the books. Join the long edges together using double-sided tape. Make the base of the bag by folding in the bottom edges as you would when wrapping a present in the usual way. Fix the base with double-sided tape.

4 Carefully slide the books out of the bag. Pinch the sides of the bag together to form a crease down the centre of each side. Hold the top edges together and punch two holes through both thicknesses of giftwrap.

YOU WILL NEED

Christmas giftwrap
A large sheet of plain paper
Pencil
Ruler
Scissors
Books to act as mould
Glue stick
Hole punch
Giftwrap ribbon
Double-sided tape

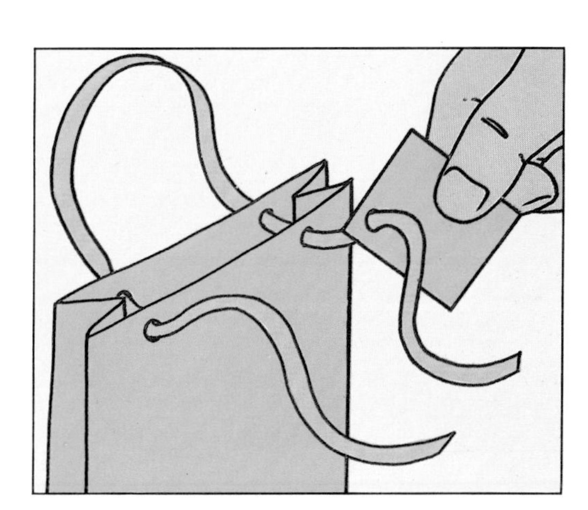

5 Cut a small square of giftwrap for a tag. Glue a square of plain paper to the back. Punch a hole in one corner of the tag and thread it on to the ribbon. Thread the ribbon through the holes in the bag to make handles and knot the ends.

SHINY SWEET SWAG

Make a decorative sweet swag from a selection of wrapped sweets, some tinsel and ribbon. Easy to make, this fun idea also provides a tasty treat when you take down your Christmas decorations – if you can wait that long!

YOU WILL NEED

2.5cm (1in) wide ribbon
Tinsel
Wrapped sweets
Stapler
Shiny giftwrap ribbon
Scissors
Card
Pen

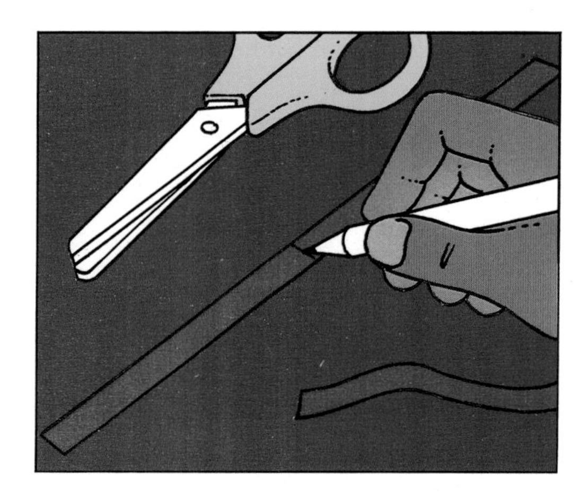

1 Cut a piece of ribbon the length you want your finished swag to be. Mark the half-way point with a pen to show where to position the centre loop.

2 Staple one end of each sweet to the ribbon. Leave a 5cm (2in) gap either side of the pen mark for the centre loop.

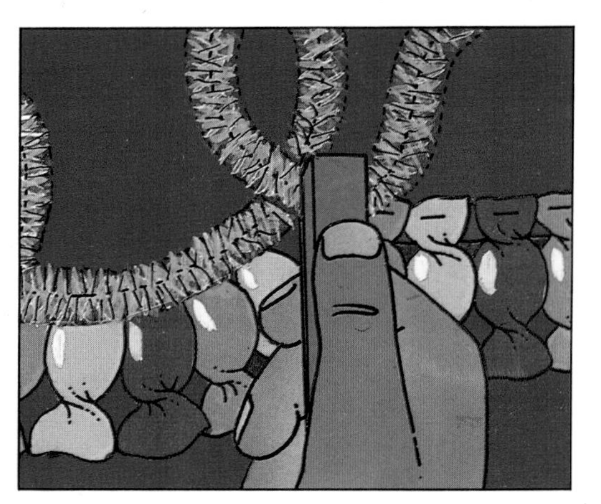

3 Make a tinsel loop, and staple to one end of the swag. Staple a long length of tinsel to the ribbon to cover the stapled ends of the sweets. Make a tinsel loop at the gap in the middle of the ribbon. Continue to staple the tinsel to the ribbon until you reach the other end. Finish with another tinsel loop.

4 Tie the giftwrap ribbon to each end of the swag and make a bow around the central loop. Pull the scissor blades along the length of the trailing ends of giftwrap ribbon to make them curl up.

5 To make the rosette decoration, cut out a circle of card. Staple tinsel around the edge of the card, leaving a loop at the top. Staple sweets and shiny ribbon to the centre of the card.

PYRAMID GIFT BAGS

These pyramid-shaped gift bags are a great idea for making gifts look extra special at Christmas. Make small bags to hang on the Christmas tree or larger ones to give as presents. Fill them to the top with sweets or tiny gifts.

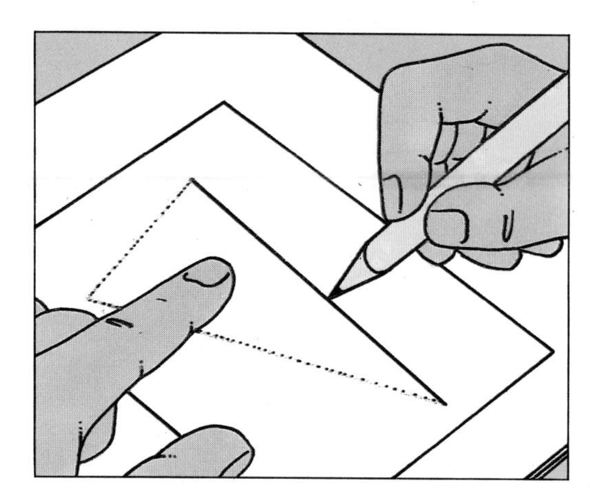

1 Using a pencil, trace either the large or the small triangle pattern on page 95. Turn the tracing over and lay it on to a piece of scrap card. Rub firmly over the outline with a pencil. The pattern will appear on the card. Cut out the shape.

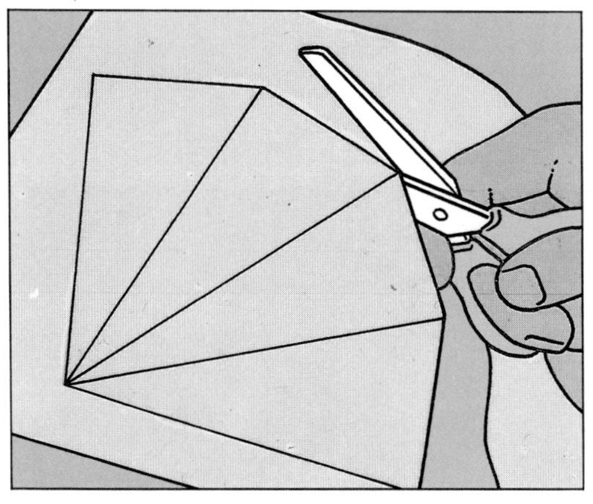

2 Lay the pattern on to the thin card and draw around it four times as shown. Keep the point in the same place each time and move the pattern along so that the long sides are edge-to-edge. Cut out the whole shape in one complete piece.

YOU WILL NEED

- Thin card
- Giftwrap
- Glue stick
- Hole punch
- Tracing paper and pencil
- Scrap card
- Scissors
- Ribbon or golden chain

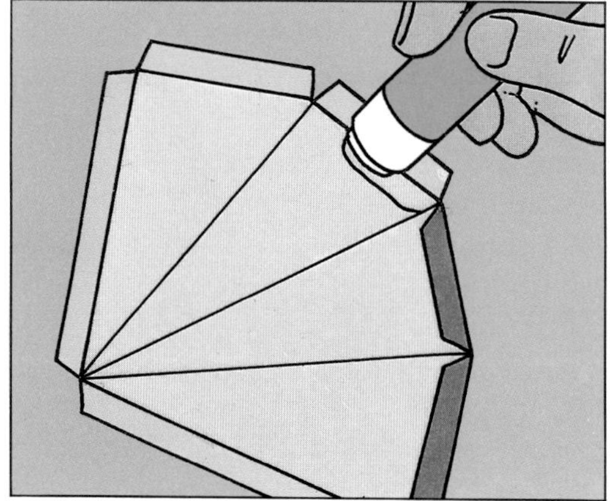

3 Coat the shape with glue and stick it to the wrong side of a sheet of giftwrap. Cut around the shape, leaving an extra 2.5cm (1in) of giftwrap all round. Fold this over and glue to the card.

4 Fold the bag shape along three sides as shown. Glue two sections together to make a pyramid shape. Leave to dry.

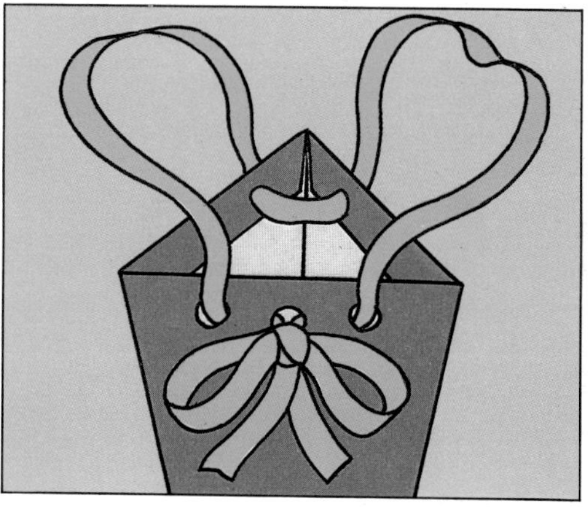

5 Punch a hole in the centre of each section at the top. Thread ribbon or a golden chain through the holes to make handles. Tie the ends together.

ICED BISCUITS

These delicious iced biscuits are great fun to make. Decorate them with icing and cake decorations like glacé cherries and angelica.

1 Turn the oven on to 180°C/ 325°F/Gas Mark 4. Wash your hands well. Put the flour and the cinnamon into a mixing bowl. Break the butter into little pieces and, using your fingers, rub it into the flour until it forms little balls.

2 Add the sugar and the egg to the mixture and mix well until it forms a thick dough. Sprinkle a clean surface with a little flour and roll out the dough with a rolling pin. Grease a baking tray with a little butter. Using biscuit cutters, cut the dough into different shapes.

SAFETY TIP: *Make sure an adult helps you when using the oven.*

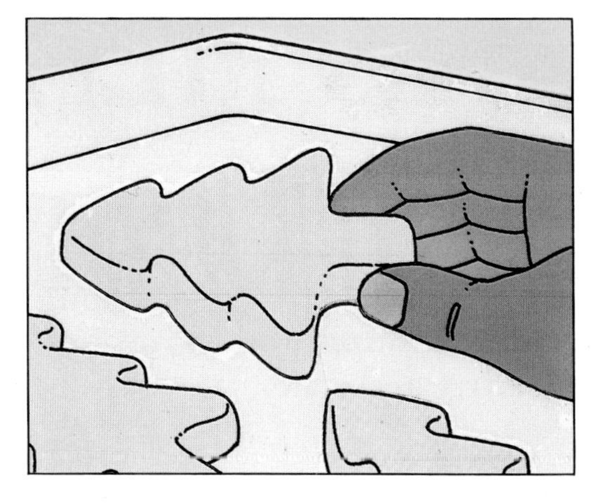

3 Carefully lift the shapes on to a baking tray. Bake the biscuits for about 15 minutes or until the edges turn golden. Wearing oven gloves, remove them from the oven and leave them to cool on a wire rack.

4 To make the icing, mix the icing sugar with 3 teaspoons of water; the icing should form a thick, smooth paste. Add a few drops of food colouring to the icing to tint it slightly.

YOU WILL NEED

150g (6oz) plain flour
2 teaspoons ground cinnamon
100g (4oz) butter
40g (1½oz) brown sugar
1 egg
100g (4oz) icing sugar
Food colouring

5 Place the biscuits on a clean, flat plate and dribble the icing over them, letting it run down the sides of the biscuits. When it has just started to set, gently press on the chopped glacé cherries and angelica. Leave the icing to set.

GINGERBREAD MEN

Delicious and fun to eat, these gingerbread men can also be hung on the Christmas tree as decorations. If you do hang them up, remember that you should eat them within a couple of days, or they will become dirty and stale.

1 Turn the oven on to 180°C/350°F/Gas Mark 4. Grease a baking tray with a little butter. Put the dry ingredients into a mixing bowl.

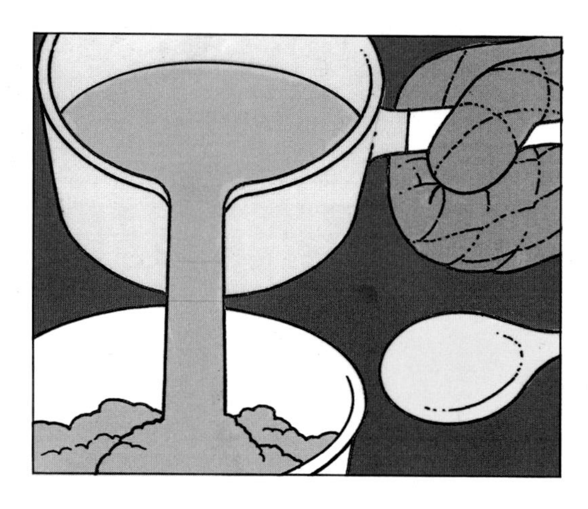

2 Put the butter, treacle and sugar in a saucepan and heat gently until they have melted. Pour the melted mixture into the bowl of dry ingredients and add the beaten egg. Mix all the ingredients together to form a ball of dough.

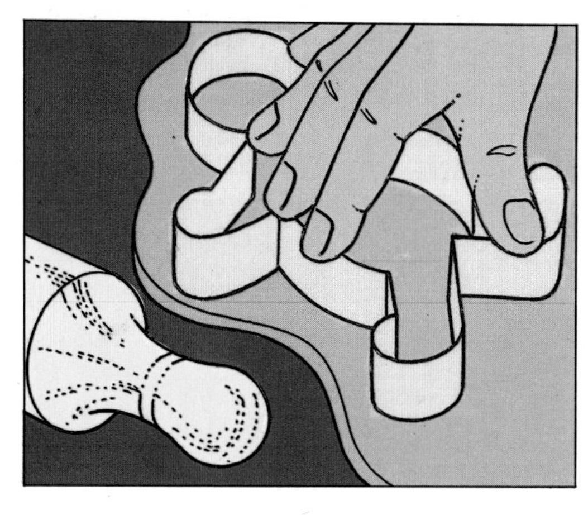

3 Sprinkle a little flour on to your work top and using a rolling pin, roll out the dough until it is about 3mm (1/8in) thick. Cut out the biscuits with a gingerbread man cutter. Transfer the shapes on to a baking tray.

4 Bake the gingerbread men for about 20 minutes, until they are brown around the edges. Wearing oven gloves, remove the tray from the oven. While the biscuits are still warm, make a hole in the top of the head using the tip of a pen or skewer.

YOU WILL NEED
250g (8oz) plain flour
1 teaspoon ground ginger
1 teaspoon bicarbonate of soda
60g (2oz) butter
60g (2oz) light brown sugar
75g (2½oz) treacle or golden syrup
1 egg, beaten
Icing pens and ribbon

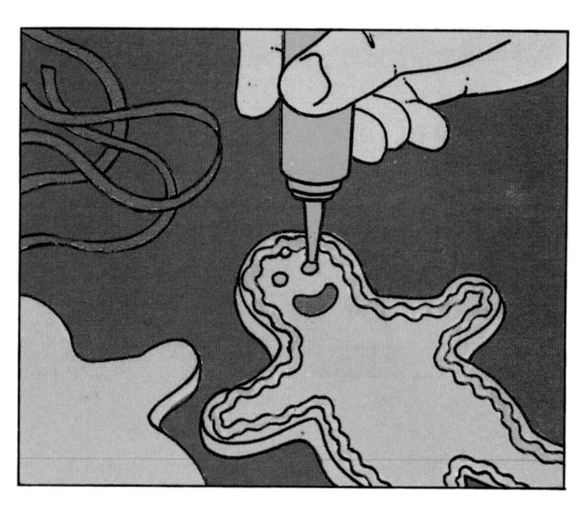

5 When the gingerbread men have cooled, use icing pens to decorate them. Tie a ribbon through the hole in the top.

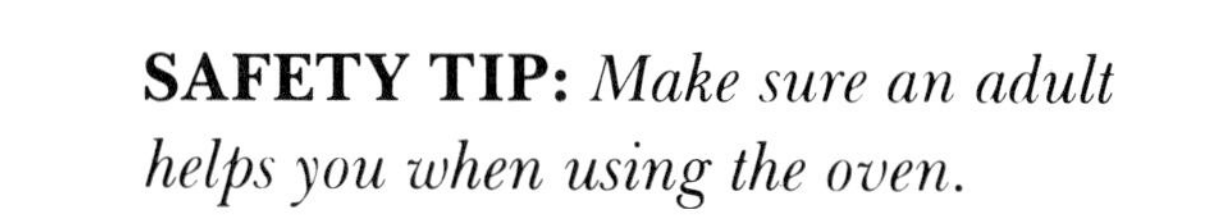

SAFETY TIP: *Make sure an adult helps you when using the oven.*

FESTIVE FUDGE

Vanilla fudge is fun to make, and quite simple. Pack it in glittery cellophane or small boxes to make a delicious Christmas present.

YOU WILL NEED

450g (1lb) caster sugar
100g (4oz) butter
425g (15oz) can condensed milk
Few drops of vanilla essence
Heavy-based, large saucepan
20cm (8in) square tin
Non-stick baking paper
Wooden spoon
Knife

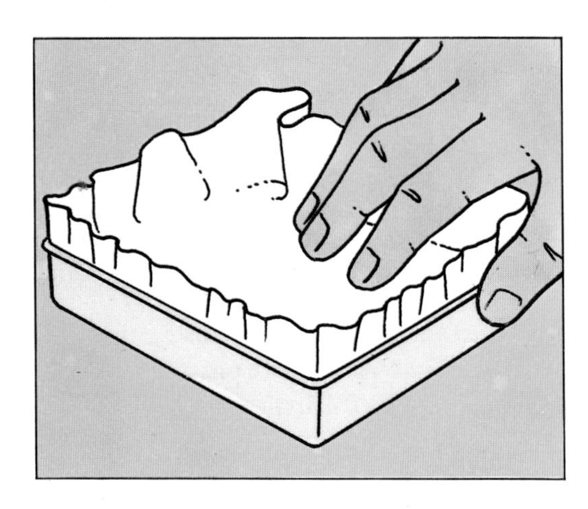

1 Line the tin with the non-stick baking paper before you start to cook. Set to one side.

2 Put the caster sugar, butter, condensed milk and vanilla essence into a large saucepan. Heat gently, stirring all the time, until the sugar has dissolved and the butter has melted.

3 Bring the mixture to the boil. Boil for 10-15 minutes, stirring continuously, until the mixture has thickened and turned a golden brown colour. Turn off the heat.

4 Pour the mixture into the tin and smooth flat. Using a knife, lightly mark squares on to the top of the fudge. Leave to cool completely before removing from the tin and cutting the fudge into squares.

SAFETY TIP: *Make sure an adult helps you when using the oven.*

SUGAR MICE

Make some colourful pink sugar mice to decorate the Christmas table or to give to friends as a sweet treat. Look out for mice-shaped moulds in larger cookery shops.

YOU WILL NEED
225g (8oz) caster sugar
2-4 teaspoons cold water
½ teaspoon red food colouring
Liquorice laces or boot lace sweets
Mixing bowl
Teaspoon
Mice-shaped moulds
Greaseproof paper

1 Put the sugar into the bowl. Mix together the food colouring and water. Slowly add it to the sugar, mixing well, to make it the consistency of damp sand.

2 Fill the mice-shaped moulds three-quarters full with the pink sugar mixture. Use the back of a teaspoon to pack the mixture down firmly.

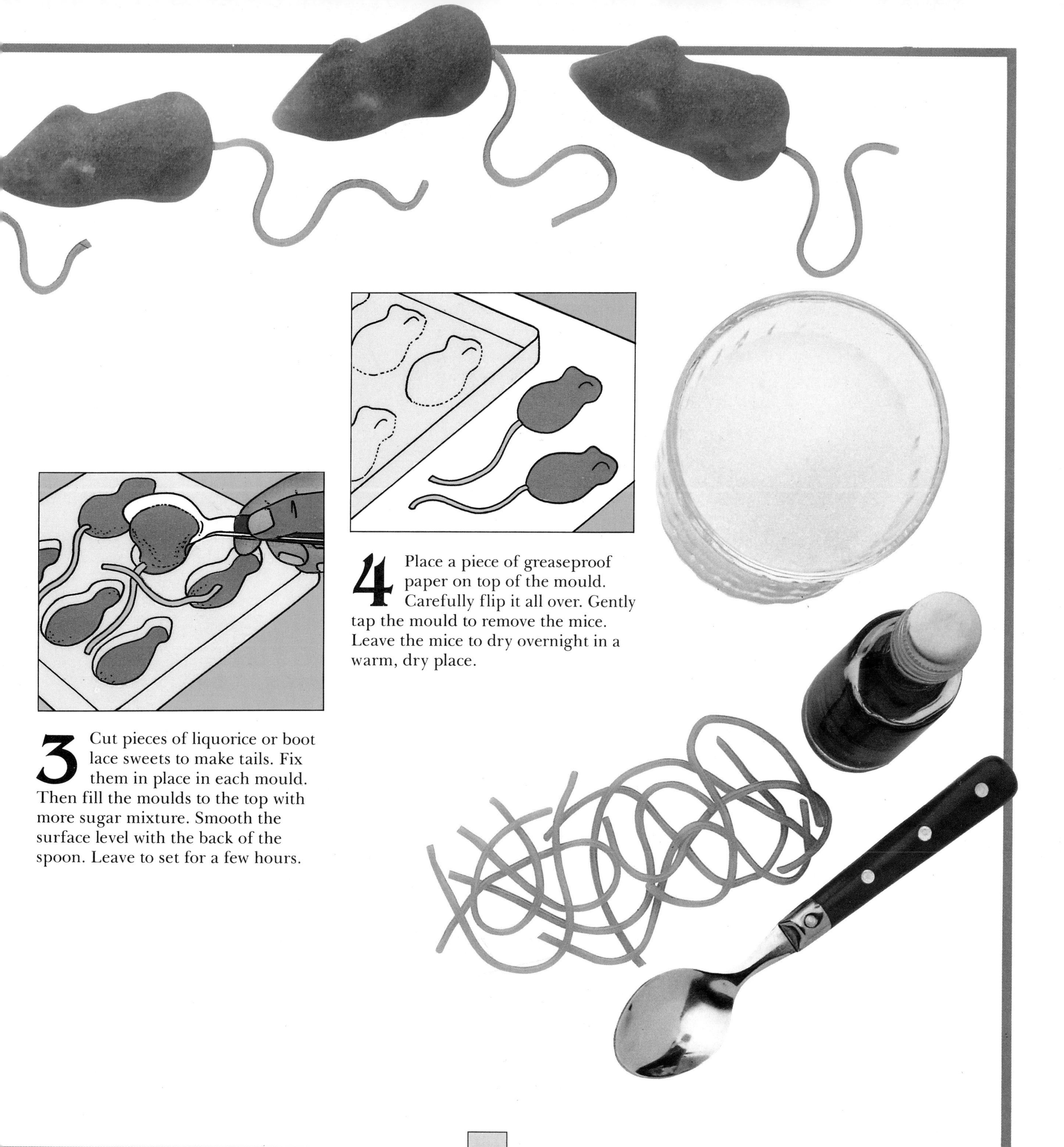

4 Place a piece of greaseproof paper on top of the mould. Carefully flip it all over. Gently tap the mould to remove the mice. Leave the mice to dry overnight in a warm, dry place.

3 Cut pieces of liquorice or boot lace sweets to make tails. Fix them in place in each mould. Then fill the moulds to the top with more sugar mixture. Smooth the surface level with the back of the spoon. Leave to set for a few hours.

PATTERNS

Some of the projects in this book are based on the patterns given on the following pages. To find out how to copy a pattern follow the step-by-step instructions given for each project.

You may want to make a pattern that you can keep to use again. To do this trace over the outline of the pattern with a pencil. Turn your tracing over and lay it on to a piece of thick card. Rub firmly over the outline with a pencil. The image will appear on the card. Cut out the shape. If you keep this pattern in a safe place, you can use it time and time again.

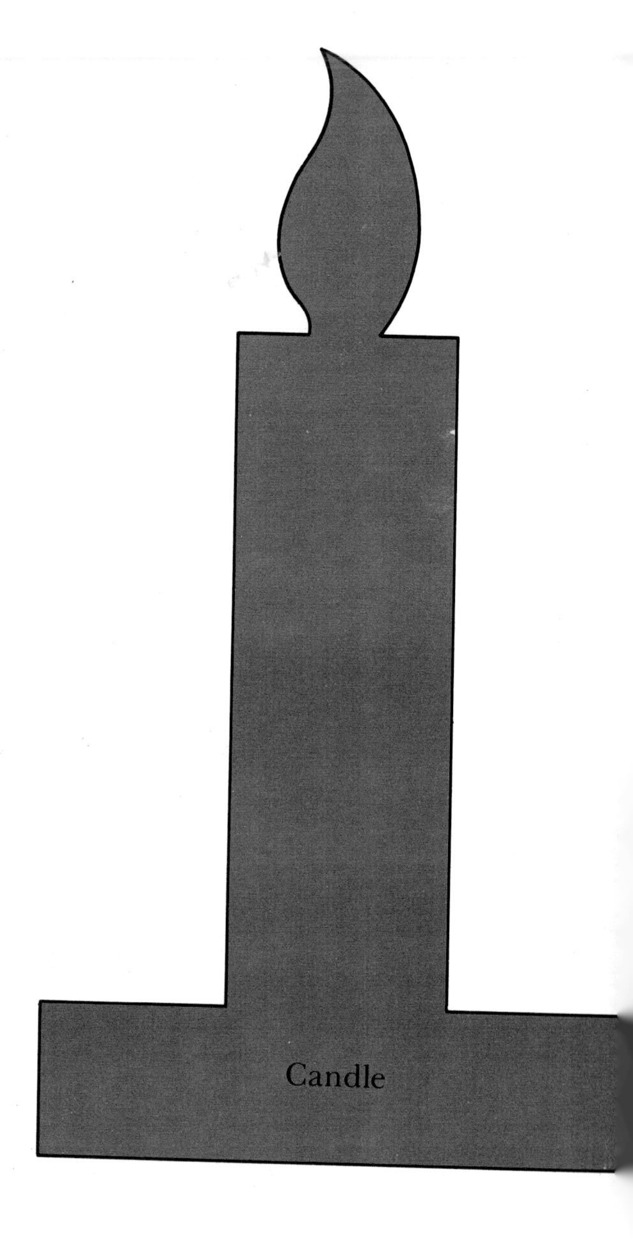

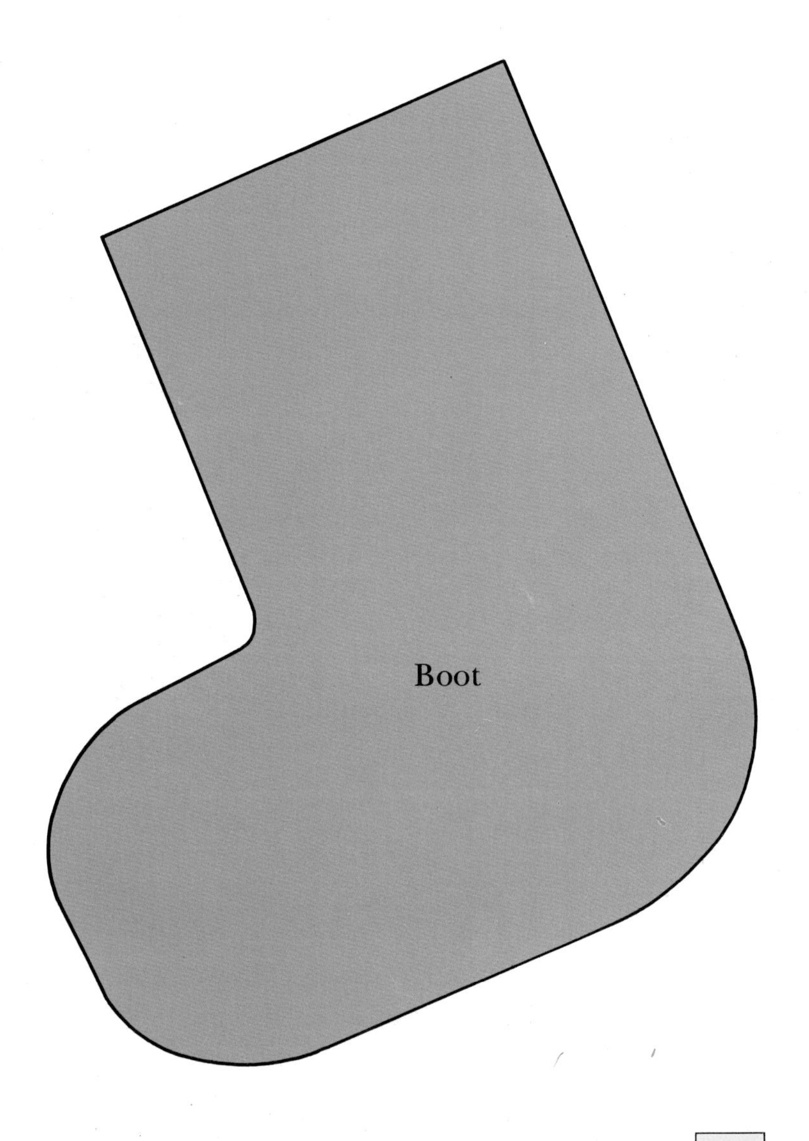

FELT TREE ORNAMENTS
Page **8**

POP-UP SANTA
Page **10**

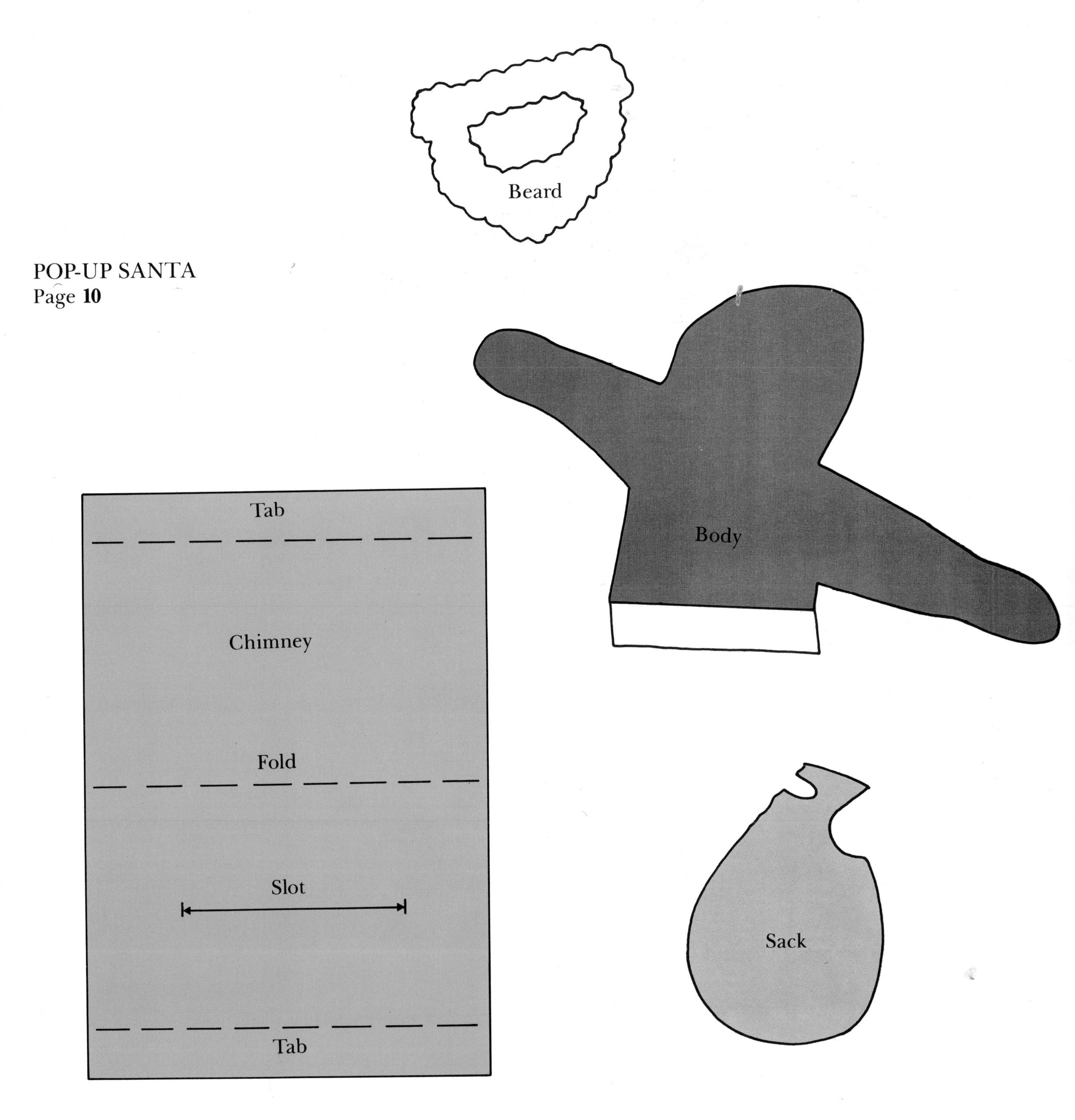

SALT-DOUGH CANDLE HOLDERS
Page 12

CHRISTMAS STOCKING
Page **14**

FABRIC CUT-OUT CARDS
Page **26**

Cone

CRÊPE PAPER TREE
Page **28**

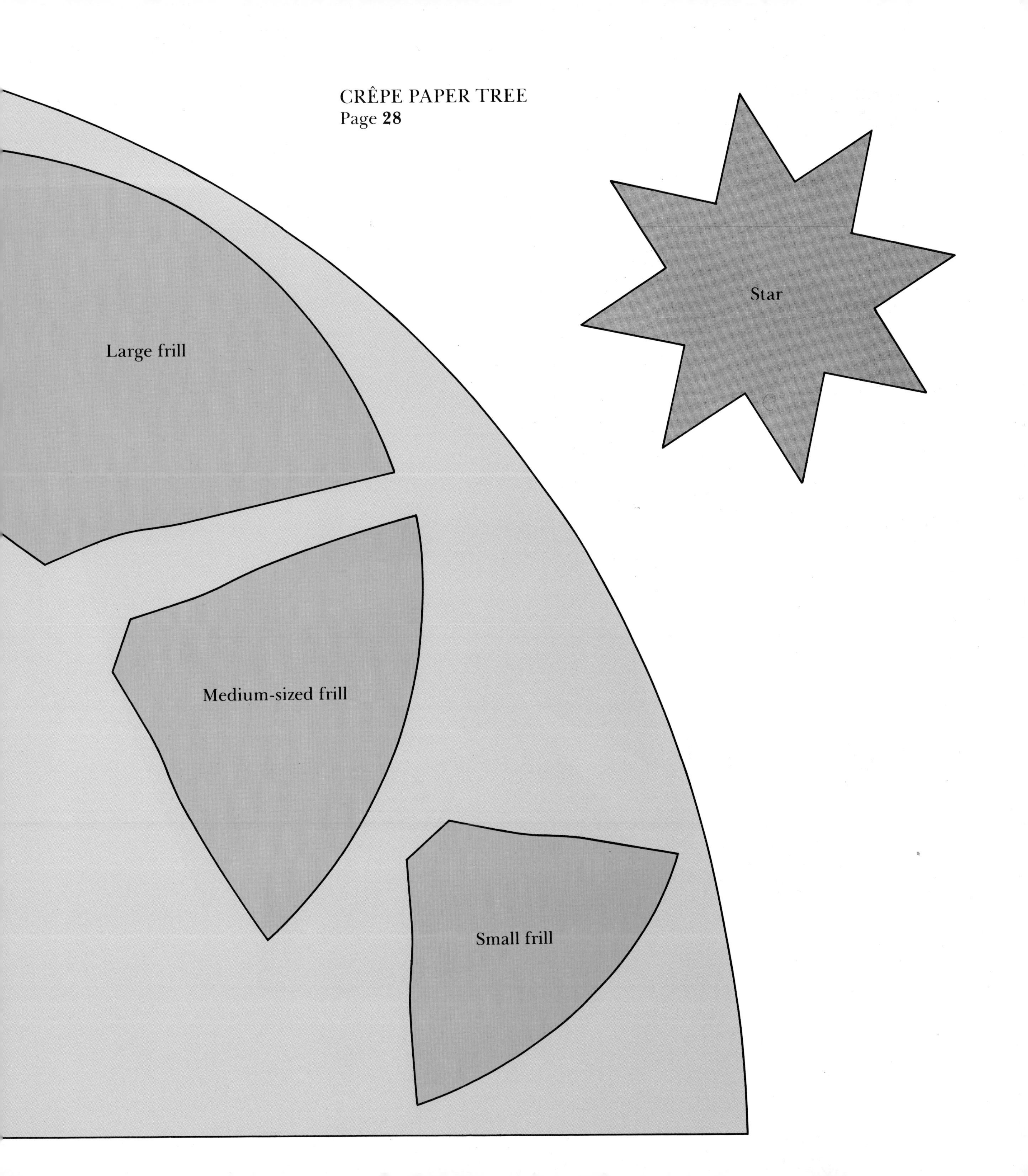

FLYING ANGELS
Page **30**

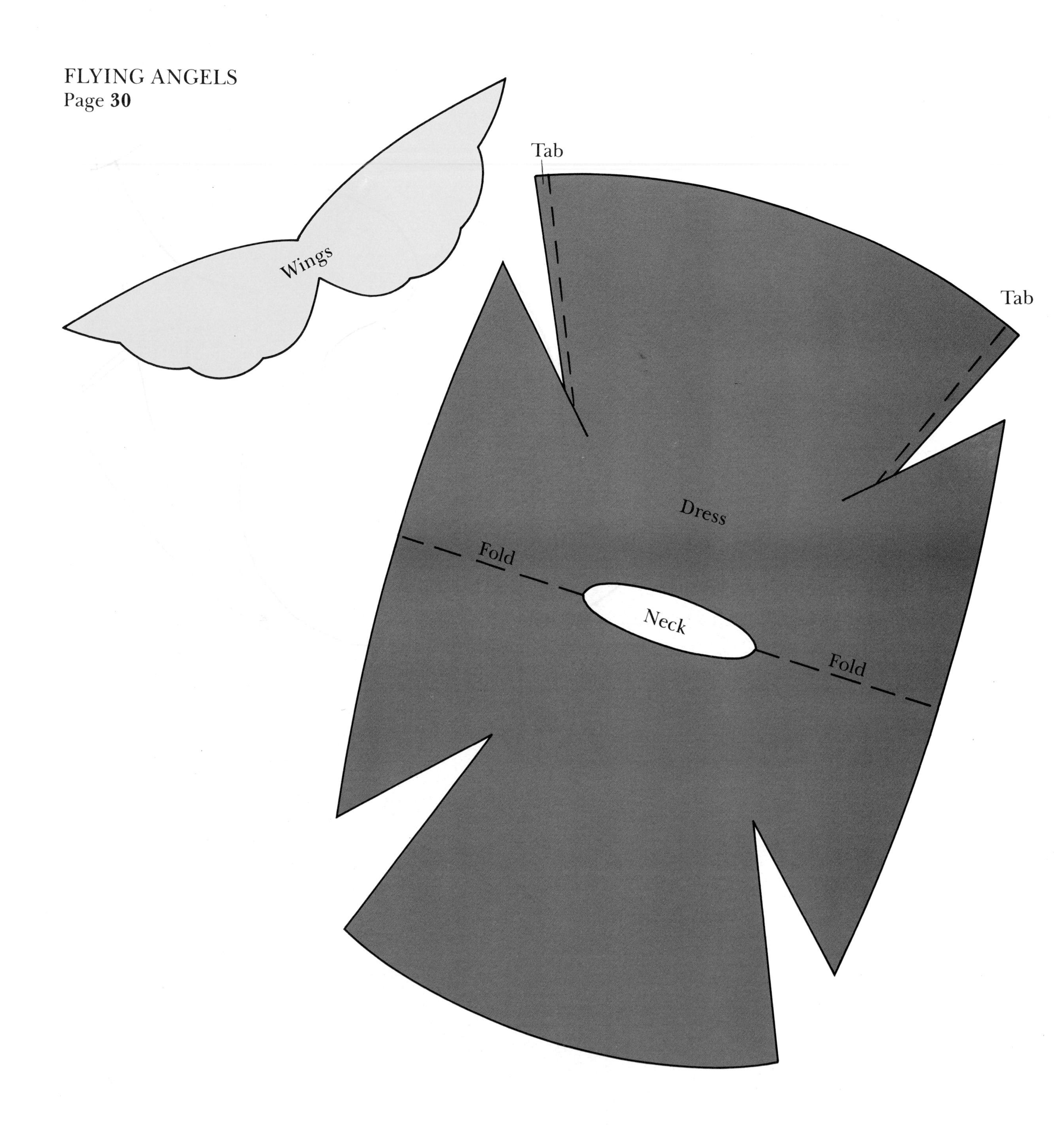

CHRISTMAS ANGEL
Page **42**

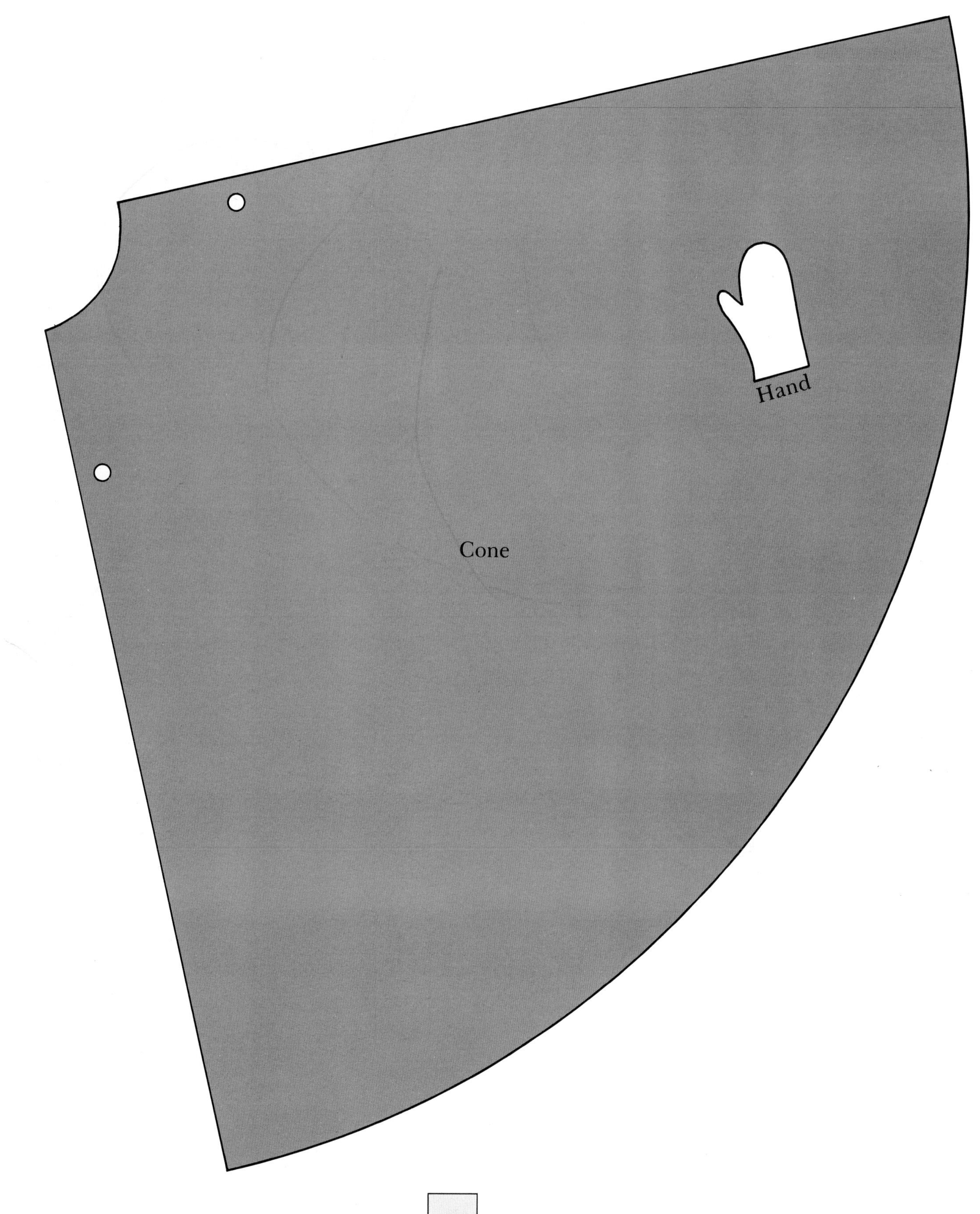

SANTA GLOVE PUPPET
Page **52**

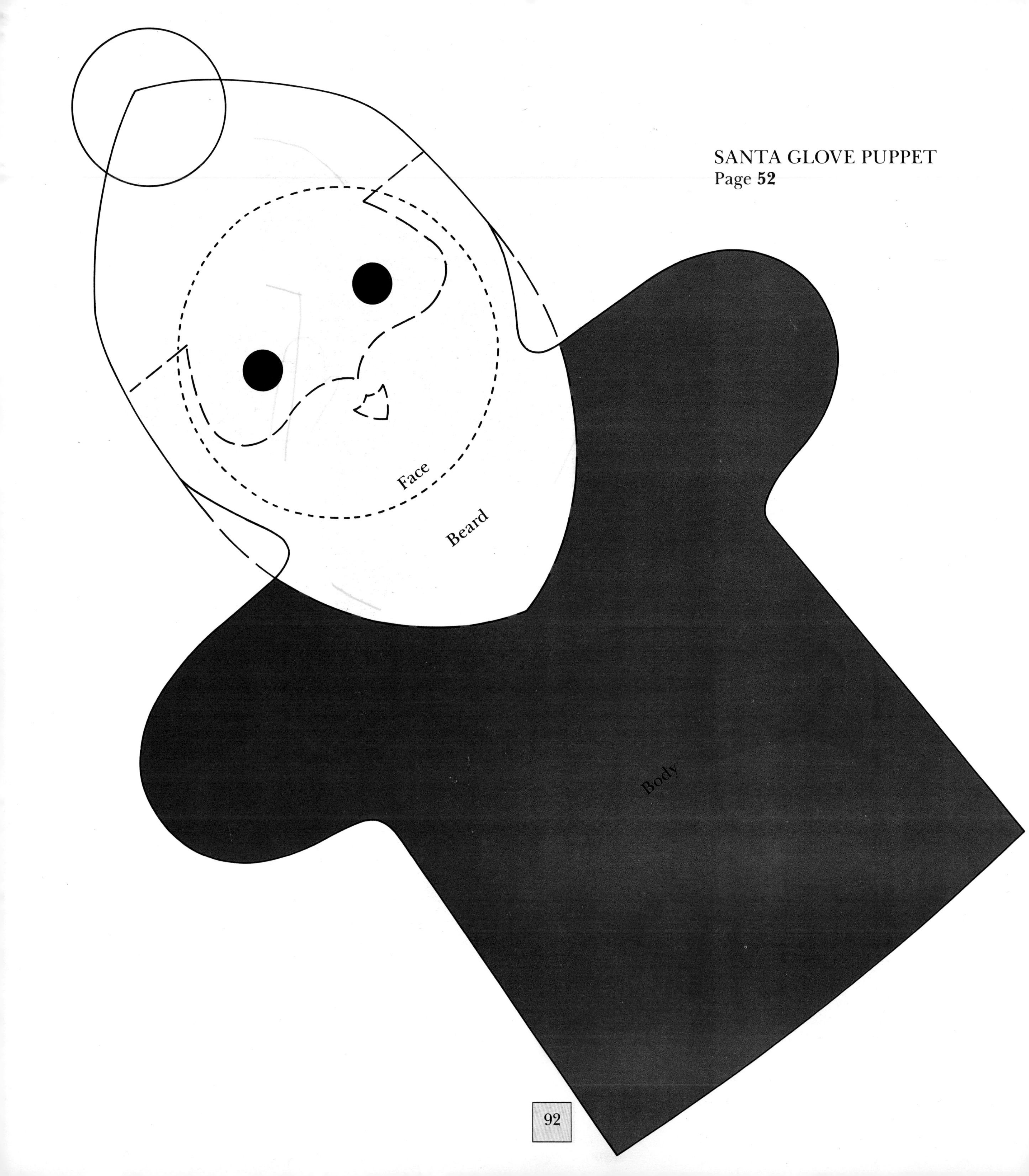

STARS AND BELLS
Page **58**

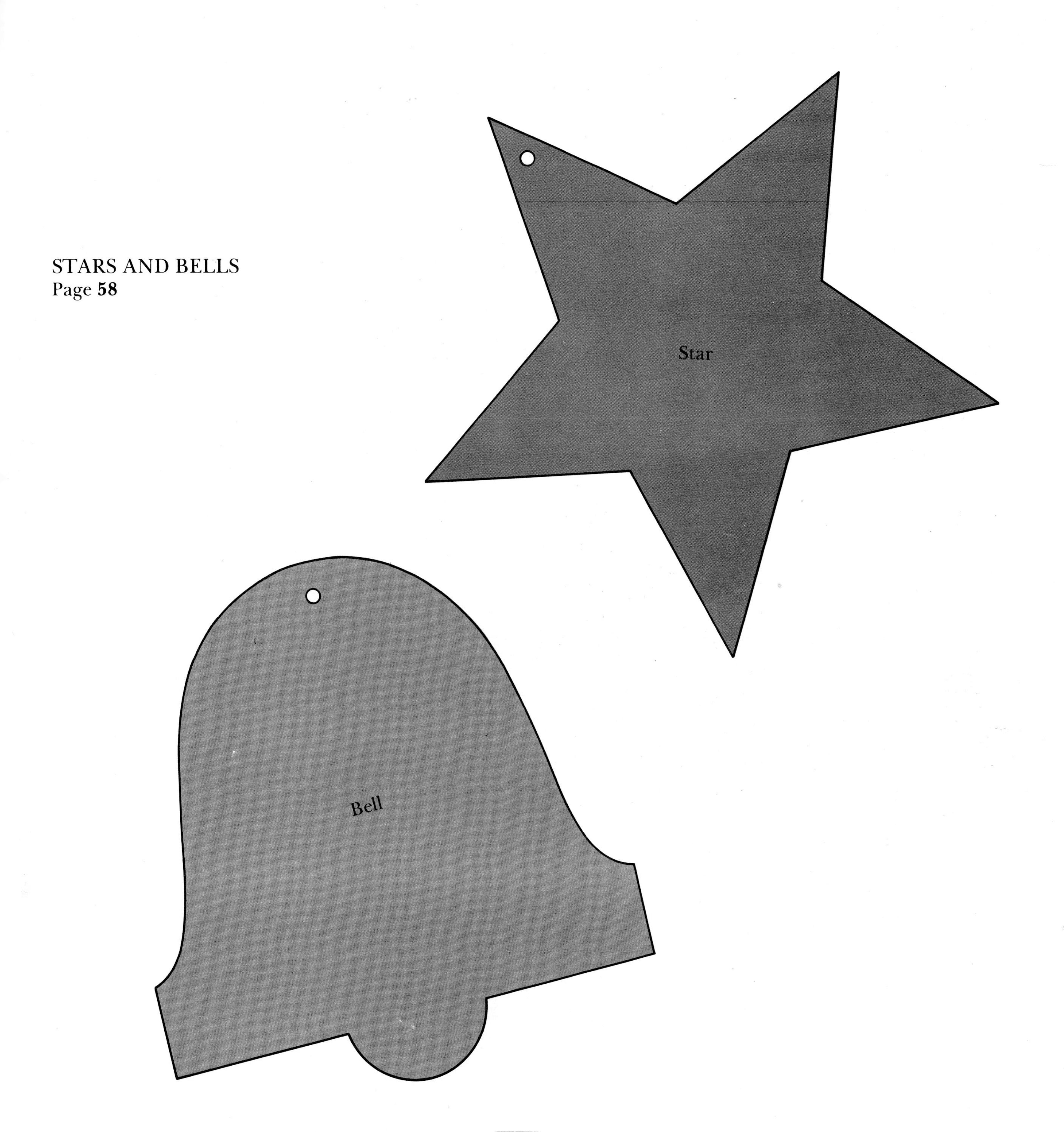

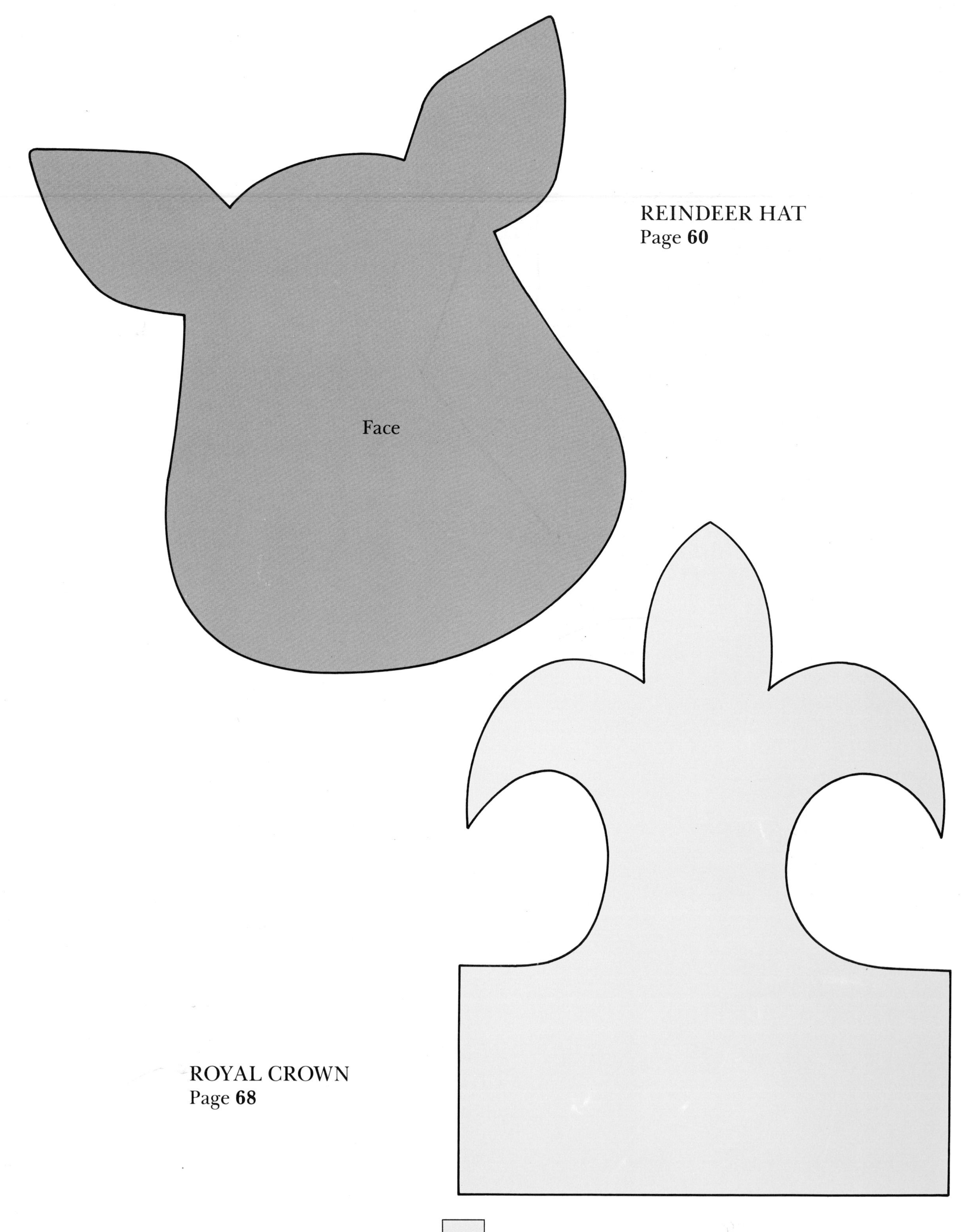

REINDEER HAT
Page **60**

ROYAL CROWN
Page **68**

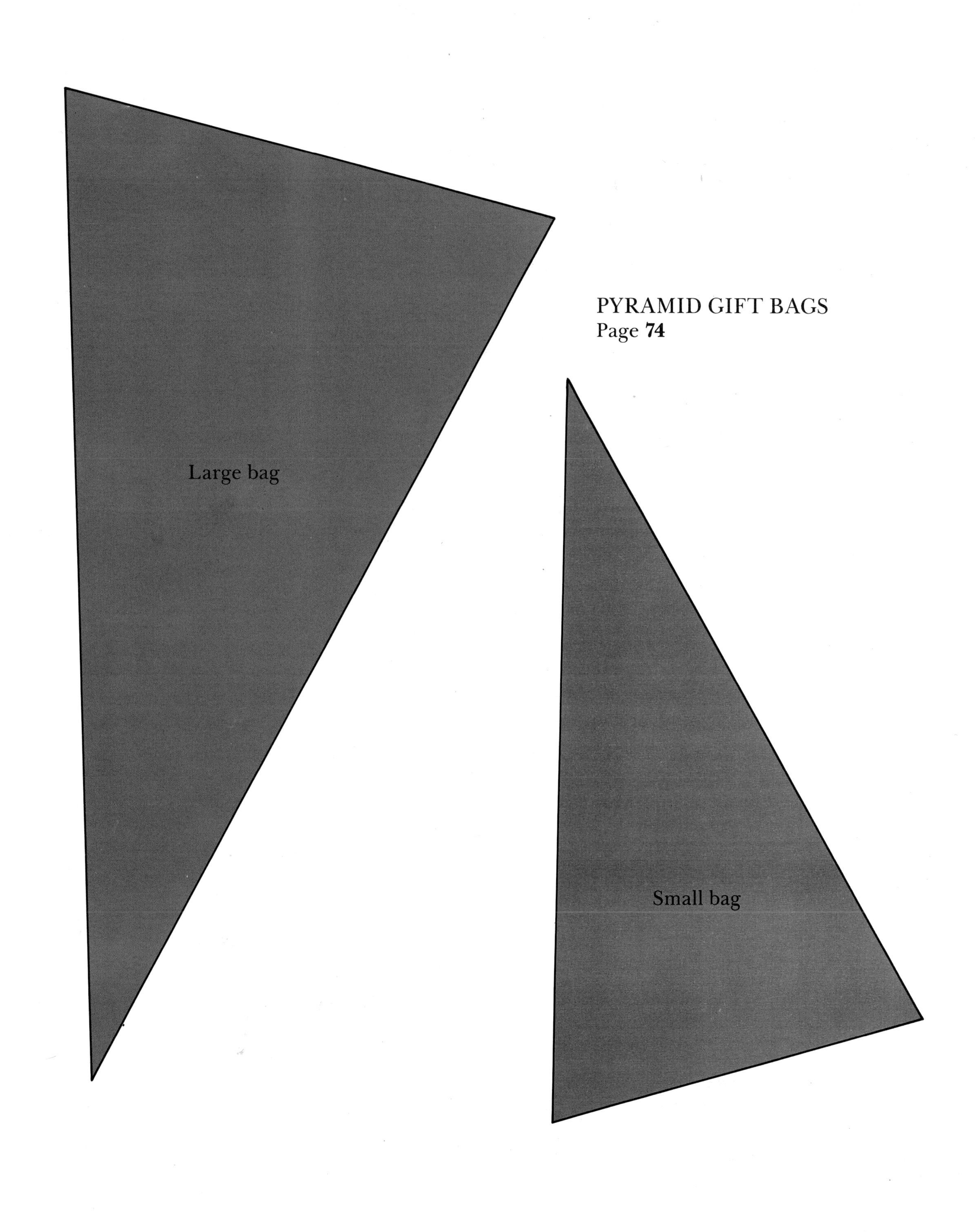

PYRAMID GIFT BAGS
Page **74**

INDEX

ACKNOWLEDGEMENT

The publishers would like to thank Hallmark Cards Ltd, Henley-on-Thames, Oxon, for their help in compiling this book.

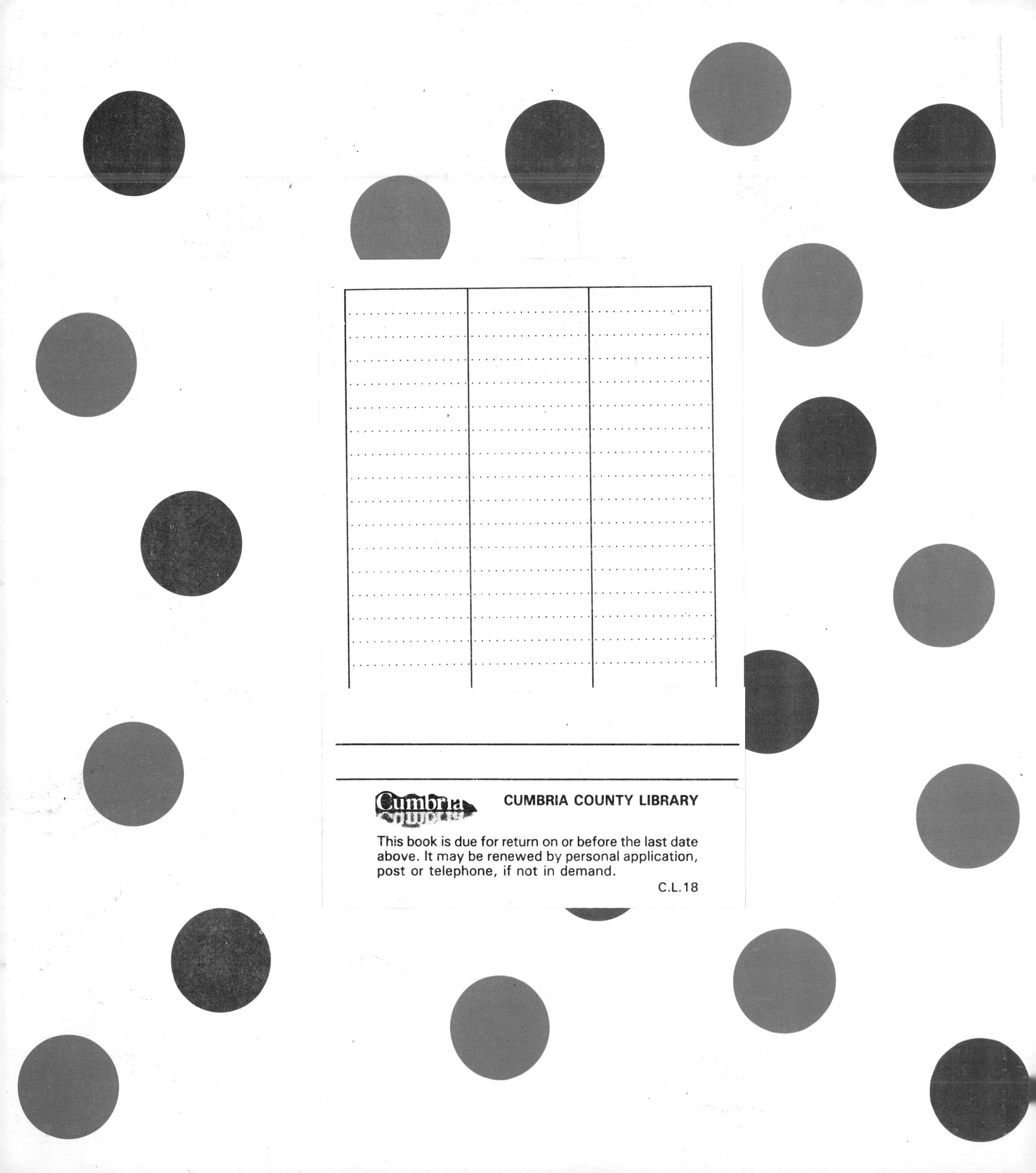